Babysitting Co-op 101

A Win-Win Childcare Solution

Samantha Fogg Nielsen
Rachel Tolman Terry

DEDICATION

To my sweet husband and family--thank you for supporting me in all of my pursuits. And to my amazing friends and the mothers in my very first babysitting co-op. *Thank You* for making our babysitting co-op such a wonderful success. I couldn't have written this book without you!

-Samantha

To Ben, Rebecca, Spencer, and Eva--thanks for your patience, support, and love. Thanks, too, to all the friends, neighbors, and relatives who have looked out for my children, taught them, and helped them to see the world as a friendly, wondrous place.

-Rachel

CONTENTS

ACKNOWLEDGMENTS

We extend special thanks to Annie McGee, Sherie Borgquist, Lana Hope, Tiffany Knowles, Anna Johnson, Sara Chandler, Abbee Hawkes, Kelly Miller, Carol Fawson, and all the friends who have worked with us in babysitting co-ops over the years. Thanks to Brittany Reese Terry for her cover photography, Jennifer Weltz and Laura Biagi for their wonderful advice, and Stephanie and Eileen Leavitt for their helpful suggestions.

INTRODUCTION

Welcome to *Babysitting Co-Op 101*! We hope this childcare solution helps you find more time: time to spend with your spouse, to run errands, and to pursue personal interests. While we may not be able to literally provide you with more hours in the day, we believe the babysitting co-op program will quickly prove to be an invaluable resource and solution in helping you find more of that precious commodity: time.

Simply put, a babysitting co-op is a formalized babysitting program consisting of parents who know one another. These parents come together to provide their babysitting services for free in a systematic and structured way. The babysitting co-op truly is a cooperative effort between individuals who share common interests, goals, and parenting styles.

The benefits of a babysitting co-op seem to be endless. While we'd like to spend more time talking about all these wonderful "extras," we feel it best to highlight the ones that hold the greatest importance for parents:

- *Creates a sense of freedom and support for parents*
- *Saves families money*
- *Eliminates the hassle of finding a sitter*
- *Offers socializing opportunities for children*
- *Provides peace of mind for parents when away*

Parents around the country have put our co-op program to the test and are responding with enthusiastic praise. Whenever we meet parents who have implemented the babysitting co-op program, the first thing we hear is, "I am so grateful for babysitting co-op!" This phrase is usually followed by, "I wish I'd known about this sooner. It would've made my life a whole lot easier."

No longer is a quiet afternoon a distant dream far off in the future. Extra cash quickly becomes increasingly available because co-op parents eliminate the need to pay for childcare expenses. Romances are rekindled through spontaneous lunch dates, and children broaden their circles of friends. All this and more has become the reality of co-op parents' everyday lives and can be a regular part of your life as well.

Samantha's friend Abbee summed up her feelings this way, "The babysitting co-op is completely guilt free! I can run to the grocery store, visit the doctor or meet my husband for lunch and not feel guilty about handing my children off to a babysitter." Another friend told us, "Babysitting co-op has helped me to maintain my sanity when the job of being a full-time parent feels overwhelming."

Yes, babysitting co-op is a guilt free, sanity-saving and cost-effective childcare solution that's fun and easy to implement. Within this book, you'll find all the tools needed to get your program up and running. Additionally, the babysitting co-op program will help you rediscover the benefits of having time on your side, time to take care of your needs and return to your family feeling refreshed and ready to go once again.

Think this sounds too good to be true? See what dozens of other parents have to say about babysitting co-op throughout the pages of this book and then decide for yourself.

Life Before Co-op
Samantha's Story

While all this sounds wonderful, things were not always so simple. Samantha still remembers the day when she realized that it was simply impossible for her to accomplish all of her activities with her little one attached to her hip. The real awakening occurred shortly after her first daughter was born. Samantha decided to get her hair cut at the beauty salon and, since she didn't have anyone to help her with Sydney, she took her along. She packed plenty of snacks and activities for her adorable toddler to enjoy and didn't think twice. She sat Sydney down on the floor next to the hairdressing chair and that was when the real chaos began.

Things were going reasonably well, at first. Samantha gave Sydney gentle directions, asking her to color mommy a pretty picture and to stay there. Well, of course it didn't work for more than two or three minutes, and it wasn't long before Sydney came up with a game plan of her own. In the middle of her haircut, Sydney decided that Samantha's purse looked far more appealing than board books, rattles and baby dolls.

Within a matter of only a few seconds, Sydney had Samantha's entire purse emptied on the floor and proceeded to eat a whole pack of gum. Samantha was concerned about Sydney ending her short life by choking on a golf ball sized wad of gum. But what was she going to do? Fortunately, Sydney quickly grew tired of each freshly chewed piece and would spit it out only to reach for a new shiny stick. Samantha was horrified! What was she thinking taking her to the salon? And, to top it all off, Samantha was in no position (literally) to be getting up and down from her chair to correct this innocent and typical toddler-like behavior.

This is when the concept of babysitting co-op was born. Samantha had heard of parents trading babysitting for one another but knew that inevitably, this trading system never really worked out well in the end. Either one parent would be late picking up her child, or maybe she would cancel at the last minute, causing the other parent to feel annoyed because she'd been waiting around her house all morning for little Tyler to show up.

No, this type of babysitting was not the answer Samantha was searching for. And she certainly did not want to bother her neighbors who'd already raised their children. They were finally at a point in life where beautiful white sofas and expensive figurines were no longer off limits. She was at a loss, and yet, it was this very dilemma that brought about one of her greatest discoveries! Babysitting co-op.

Rachel's Story

We'll leave Samantha for a few minutes to recover from the trauma of that day and follow Rachel to the dentist's office where she sits in the waiting room with her 6-month-old son Spencer. He looks so cute sitting there in his little car seat, all bundled up in a fleece blanket. But here's how Rachel remembers it.

The hygienist called her back into the exam room and looked a little surprised when she saw the car seat hooked onto Rachel's arm, but politely, she didn't say anything. The hygienist just oohed and aahed over the baby like people do in places where babies aren't normally seen.

Rachel set the car seat down and lay back on the dentist's chair, hoping this would be a quick visit. As soon as the hygienist turned on that saliva-sucking hoses, little Spencer scrunched his face up and let out a wail. The hygienist turned off the hose and said, "Do you want to pick him up?" Rachel did, and it was obvious that the only thing he wanted to do in the whole world was to nurse.

To make an embarrassing story short, Rachel ended up nursing him under a blue paper bib while she got her teeth scraped by the smirking hygienist—it was the only way she could keep him from crying.

As Rachel packed up the diaper bag and tucked Spencer back into his seat, she apologized to the hygienist and promised she would never bring him again. "That would be a good idea," the woman said.

Rachel meant what she said; she wouldn't take a nursing infant to the dentist's office again, but that would mean she'd have to find a sitter. And paying for a babysitter while you're paying the dentist is a bitter pill to swallow. She resolved to find a better way.

Today's Parents – Always on the Go

Do you have stories like these? We have a feeling you might, since you've picked up this book. Such experiences prompt action. You just can't go on subjecting yourself, your children, and others, like hair stylists and dental hygienists, to such situations. If you don't have a plan for this sort of thing, you'll end up taking them along, much to your regret in some instances.

Today's parents are always on the go. The popular term "soccer mom" is a phrase that depicts the busy lifestyles parents adopt when children come into the picture. As parents, we think it's fair to say that we all love our children and wants what's best for them. This is why we're more than happy to cart them off to soccer practice twice a week, plus games on Saturdays. We make cookies for the preschool Halloween party and then rush home to make sure that our own ghosts and goblins are safely escorted around the neighborhood for trick-or-treating. With all this activity underway, we soon realize how quickly we can lose ourselves in the process of managing our families, always putting our needs aside, or at the very least, to the bottom of the list.

However, today's parents still have to visit the dentist and see the doctor occasionally. And although tagging along with dad to an appointment with the tax accountant might be educational for the little ones, it's really much better if they're not there. Some things are just meant to be handled on your own. Not too surprisingly, we're sure you'd agree that there's probably a long list of things you wish you could do by yourself just so you can catch up with your own thoughts.

So what do you do with your children when you really need to go somewhere by yourself? The teenagers in the neighborhood are usually at school during office hours, and even if they are available to watch your kids, you have to, you know, pay them – with hard, cold cash. While some areas have drop-in daycares that can be used on a fly-by basis, your children may not feel comfortable in such places. They likely won't know the other children, and you may not know the care givers working that day. Additionally, you won't be able to help monitor the activities, television programs or values that your children are exposed to in such an unknown environment.

This is where babysitting co-op steps in. No longer will you have to worry about finding a babysitter in the middle of the day so you can get to an appointment, and say goodbye to having to ask (or bribe) the neighbor next door to let your little one come over for a play date.

As a co-op parent, all you need to do is look at your co-op calendar, make a call, and schedule some babysitting time with another co-op parent you already know and trust. Your children get to enjoy an afternoon of carefree playtime with their friends instead of escorting you to and from your activities. When you return to pick up your child everyone is happy. By utilizing the babysitting co-op, you've saved yourself not only time and money but a whole lot of stress as well.

The babysitting co-op program is one of the most effective babysitting solutions you'll ever find. It's easy to set up, self-maintaining, and tremendous fun for both the parents and the children. In short, babysitting co-op creates a win-win situation for everyone involved.

Babysitting Co-op is Born

Initially, when Samantha realized there had to be a practical solution to her childcare dilemma, she sat down with a friend and pulled a few concepts together. They knew that it would be unrealistic to trade cash, so they decided to trade tickets instead. They set up some specific rules, printed up a calendar, and started experimenting with different scheduling techniques and shifts. Finding a few friends to join their babysitting co-op was easy, so they scheduled a meeting and put their plan into motion.

With all the interest, Samantha knew she'd hit on something great. It was working! Over the ten years since that initial co-op was organized, Samantha has fine-tuned the system so that it runs like a well-oiled machine. She's helped set up dozens of additional babysitting co-ops for other parents who need childcare alternatives for times when they can't sanely take their children along.

Within a short period of time, complete strangers were calling, wanting to find out how to set up a co-op of their own. Is it hard to implement? How many tickets do I start with? What do you do if a parent is late picking up their child? I'd like to share this program with my cousin who lives in California. Do you have anything written down that I can send her? All these questions led to the conclusion that there is a real need for this information to be shared with parents everywhere.

But the middle of the day wasn't the only time when parents need babysitting. Rachel and her husband found that going out on dates was getting really expensive, even if they only wanted to play tennis or go for a walk. The teenage girls in the neighborhood were charging astronomical hourly rates and walking around sporting Burberry sunglasses and Kate Spade handbags. It was time to opt out of that system. So Rachel talked to her next-door neighbor Kelly and came up with a date night babysitting co-op program of her own.

Rachel figured the co-op would be seen as a good thing by the kids as well as the adults. Each couple would have a regularly scheduled date night that offered flexible hours to accommodate different activities such as concerts, plays, dinner, and movies. Rachel and her husband got really excited about the prospect of spending their entertainment money on actual entertainment instead of just babysitting fees. Within a matter of weeks, Rachel realized that she'd found a way to really start enjoying date nights once again.

Get the Most from *Babysitting Co-Op 101*

Rest assured – everything is here. We wrote this book with the express purpose of providing you with a ready-to-go babysitting co-op program. All the tools you need to successfully create your own babysitting co-op are found within the following pages. We've included details such as how to organize your first meeting, create and utilize the co-op tickets, and set a schedule that compliments the needs of your group. We've also included tips and techniques that will keep your co-op running efficiently.

At the end of each chapter you'll find a chapter summary, making it easy for you to stay on track. We've even included a chapter containing all the templates and forms you'll need to get your co-op program up and running: templates such as an agenda for your planning meetings, calendars for your schedules, and medical release forms for each child in your co-op. So as you're reading through the chapters, don't worry about taking notes or creating to-do lists. Take your time to enjoy the material and capture the concepts. We've taken all the guess work out of the program.

In addition to covering the logistics, we've included chapters filled with quick and easy activities and snacks for the days when you're on duty. You'll also find practical safety tips and first-aid advice. We've even made it a point to include kid-friendly dinner menus and a list of entertaining movies for your weekend co-op shift.

We recommend that you read each chapter in *Babysitting Co-Op 101* in sequential order. Throughout the book, we build upon concepts discussed in earlier chapters. You'll have a greater understanding of how to best utilize and implement the material if you first have a solid understanding of the basic co-op concepts and practices.

Finally, know that we are here to help you every step of the way. We are genuinely interested in seeing your babysitting co-op become an invaluable asset for you and your co-op members. With this in mind, we've established a blog so you can reach us with questions and concerns or simply share a heartwarming "co-op moment" that brightened your day. Visit our blog at baby-sittingco-op.blogspot.com and take advantage of learning from other co-op member's experiences.

We have high hopes for you as you start your own babysitting co-op journey. We know you'll gain as much benefit from this program as we have. You'll join many parents who have made this program an integral part of their parenting experience. Soon, you too will be echoing the sentiments Heather shares: "Babysitting co-op has truly changed my life. I am a better mother because now I have time to rediscover some of my hobbies or quite simply do the grocery shopping by myself. My children love spending time with their friends and can't wait for it to be our co-op day. The best part of the program is that through the years, I've also built a wonderful network of moms who are also my friends."

Don't wait another minute. Jump in! We're with you.

PART I

THE FUNDAMENTALS

CHAPTER 1
DEFINITION OF A BABYSITTING CO-OP

What is a Babysitting Co-op?

As a parent, you can appreciate how hard it is to accomplish everyday tasks such as grocery shopping, running to the bank, or getting the oil changed with your children in tow. Not only do these errands tend to take longer when kids come along, but they can end up costing more money as well.

A babysitting co-op is a formalized babysitting program consisting of parents who know and trust one another and also share the same parenting philosophies. These parents come together to provide babysitting services for free within a structured framework. It is truly a cooperative effort between individuals who want their children to be cared for in a safe and known environment while they're away.

The babysitting co-op operates on a ticket exchange system versus a cash-based system. These tickets then act as the co-op's form of currency, in which time is accounted for and exchanged. As you can imagine, this system saves families a tremendous amount of money that can then be redirected toward other areas of need. The more you babysit, the more tickets you'll accrue. Accumulating tickets enables you to secure babysitting hours with other co-op members that you can then spend for your children. The co-op program is based upon the principle of supply and demand. The Ticket Exchange portion of the program will be explained in greater depth in Chapter Four.

Another unique feature to the babysitting co-op is that shifts are set for specific time periods on specific days of the week. These shifts are then projected out a few months in advance. Prearranged shifts allow members of the co-op to make plans weeks in advance without having to worry about finding a babysitter. Believe us, this is a huge benefit, and it's one of the most valuable aspects of your babysitting co-op program. We'll explore this feature more in depth in Chapter Five.

What are the Benefits to Co-op?

Families derive different benefits from participating in a babysitting co-op depending on their particular needs and situations. That said, we've found that the following benefits are universal:

- Creates a sense of freedom and support for parents – parents now have increased opportunities for quality time.
- Saves families money – co-op parents exchange their time on a ticket versus a cash basis.
- Eliminates the hassle of finding a sitter – built-in babysitting is just a phone call away.
- Offers socializing opportunities for children – kids enjoy the company of a wider circle of friends.
- Provides peace of mind for parents – children receive safe, competent and reliable care from parents they know and trust.

Here are some comments from parents who have participated in babysitting co-ops and come to appreciate the benefits:

"Staying at home with my children is a high priority for our family. While I thoroughly enjoy being a full time mom, my profession doesn't generate additional income. Having a babysitting co-op available to our family has helped us save money, which we then are able apply toward other needs." *Sara Chandler, Mother of Three*

"I am a mother of three and operate my own home based business. Prior to joining a babysitting co-op, finding quiet time in which to conduct conference calls or work on proposals was a real challenge. I've been involved in my babysitting co-op group for almost two years and love the freedom and flexibility it affords me. Thanks to our babysitting co-op, I am now able to take care of my business without interruptions while my children get to play with their friends. The babysitting co-op has eliminated my need for daycare: saving our family a significant amount of money. Contributing eight hours of my time toward babysitting for the co-op is a small tradeoff when compared to the numerous benefits the babysitting co-op program provides." *Anna Johnson, Mother of Three*

"By implementing the guidelines found in this book, I was able to successfully start my own babysitting co-op. The book is very clear and easy to understand. The authors did a great job explaining every aspect of the co-op program and in answering my questions. I was able to easily adapt different aspects of the babysitting co-op program to fit the needs of my individual group. The examples and sample material, which are provided, are very helpful. I highly recommend Babysitting Co-Op 101 to anyone who's interested in finding a fun and easy childcare solution." *Tiffany Knowles, Mother of Four*

As you can see, the babysitting co-op has helped each of these parents find a unique answer to their individual needs. The babysitting co-op truly is a win-win program for everyone involved.

Is Babysitting Co-op Right for Me?

Determining whether or not babysitting co-op is the right childcare solution for you is an important question to consider. While babysitting co-op is a wonderful childcare solution for many, it does require some time and a certain level of commitment from all of its members. The babysitting co-op program seems to best fit parents who are able to stay at home full time with their children or work on a part-time basis, although families with two working parents find that participating in a weekend babysitting co-op can fit their schedules well.

The reasons that parents participate in co-op programs vary tremendously. Some parents view co-op as a way to find more time to pursue interests and hobbies; others consider co-op an essential part of their lives because it enables them to earn additional income for their families by working part-time or running a business from home without having to pay for childcare. Some stay-at-home parents feel a desire for a more social interaction, for both themselves and their children, and babysitting co-op fills that need. While the needs of each parent are as unique as they are, the babysitting co-op program can complement a variety of situations.

Common Characteristics of Co-op Parents:

- Like to save money
- Have young children who aren't enrolled in school
- Operate a home-based business
- Work part-time hours outside of the home
- Live away from relatives who could assist with childcare
- Need additional support as a single parent
- Attend school on a part time basis
- Volunteer in schools, church organizations, community events, etc.
- Home school children
- Assist in medical care for aging parents or other relatives
- Pursue individual interests and hobbies regularly
- Seek socializing opportunities for children
- Have an only child who needs greater interaction with other children
- Supervise children's associations
- Desire safe, competent, reliable care in a known and trusted environment

Co-op and Working Parents

Some may wonder if a working parent can also be involved in a babysitting co-op program. This depends upon the nature of your job and personal situation. For parents who work part-time hours, co-op can prove to be a very valuable solution because it eliminates paying for childcare. In fact, throughout the years, we've seen a number of parents use the co-op program as their childcare solution rather than an in-home babysitter or a daycare center.

Let's take a look at Emily's situation. Emily is the mother of three children ages seven, four and two. When Emily first decided to go back to work as a teacher's aide, she and her husband sat down to determine if returning to work was the right decision for their family. Could she earn enough after taxes, commuting, and daycare fees to make her time away from her family worth the cost? Emily knew that paying for daycare was not an option. By the time she covered all the incidentals, plus babysitting expenses for two children, she'd have next to nothing to show for her efforts.

This is when Emily called her friend Michelle who had once told her about the babysitting co-op program. She recalled hearing a few details about the program, but what really stood out in Emily's mind was the fact that babysitting co-op didn't incur any financial costs. After making a quick phone call, Emily decided to start her own babysitting co-op program with friends from her neighborhood. She could schedule her kids to play at another co-op mom's home while she was at work and actually help with the family's finances. Additionally, when she and her husband sat down to do the math, they quickly realized that co-op was the right answer for them.

Daycare vs. Co-op: A Financial Comparison

Hourly Difference = $3.75
*Co-op Parents Profit **35% More** Per Hour Than Parents Utilizing Daycare Programs.*

Scenario #1	Scenario #2
Working Parent Paying Daycare	*Working Parent Using Co-op*
$ 12.50 (hourly wage)	$ 12.50 (hourly wage)
x 8 (hours per day)	x 8 (hours per day)
$100.00 (earnings per day)	$100.00 (earnings per day)
$100.00 (earnings per day)	$100.00 (earnings per day)
- $ 15.00 (15% taxes)	- $ 15.00 (15% taxes)
$ 85.00 (total per day)	$ 85.00 (total per day)
$85.00 (earnings per day)	*Active Co-op Parent*
- $30.00 (daycare expense for 1 child per day)	*No Daycare Expenses Incurred*
$55.00 (total per day)	
$55.00 (earnings per day)	$85.00 (earnings per day)
÷ 8 (hours per day)	÷ 8 (hours per day)
$6.87 (hourly wage)	$10.62 (hourly wage)
Net Hourly Income = $6.87	Net Hourly Income = $10.62

How Do I Find Parents to Join My Co-op?

Finding parents to join your new venture is not as difficult as it seems. Your first step should be to look at the friends you socialize with on a regular basis. If you allow your children to play with your friend's children, then these parents are probably good candidates to start with. But remember that sticking with your closer friends is not the only avenue to explore when forming your co-op.

There are several ways to go about finding parents to join in your babysitting co-op. You probably have a larger network of friends than you realize. We've met a number of great parents through activities such as church organizations, preschool, sports teams, dance lessons, play groups, jobs, book clubs, library hour and volunteering committees. If you're having difficulties identifying who you'd like to invite into your co-op, start by making a list. We're sure you'll be surprised by your results. In fact, one mom said, "Co-op has helped me to establish friendships with parents that I may have never known."

The important thing to remember is that when you're inviting parents to join co-op, you want to invite people you know and trust. It's best to invite parents who are reliable and share the same values, parenting styles, and home environments. This point can't be stressed enough. This simple but valuable piece of advice will significantly reduce the chances of conflict within your babysitting co-op. While we certainly don't like hurting people's feelings or excluding individuals from an activity, the co-op is more than just a social club. There are some parents who won't meet the standards you have in mind for your particular co-op. And when it comes to your children, your comfort level with a caregiver and the inherent safety of the home should always be the first and foremost consideration.

Babysitting co-ops have been started with as few as four members and as many as twelve to fourteen members. Starting a babysitting co-op with more than fourteen members can be difficult to manage. While larger groups provide parents with more shifts to choose from, you may find that not all of the shifts are being used. As a result, some parents may have decreased opportunities to earn tickets. Finally, the number of children that a parent has should not influence a parent's eligibility in joining the babysitting co-op.

Kids Love Co-op, Too

Everyone knows that other people's toys are more fun than their own. Ask any child. And after your kids have been in co-op for a while, you'll see that other people's toys are not the only reason they like co-op.

Rachel's son Spencer has two sisters and no brothers, so he craves the companionship of other boys. He counts the minutes until he can go spend the afternoon at a home with boys. And when a boy is coming over to his house, Spencer eagerly gets his cars and rockets ready for someone who will truly appreciate them.

Even more desperate for kids' company than Spencer are children with no siblings at all. One mom of an only child recently told us, "It's so good for Riley to have this chance to socialize with other kids in an informal, home setting. He learns so much in the interactions and loves to feel like one of the crowd." Only children miss out on some intimate interaction with other children, so co-op gives them a sibling-like experience.

At other people's homes, your children will be exposed to many different things, and their world views will be expanded, even if only a little bit. They'll play new games that you don't play at your house. They'll try different foods and learn to appreciate (maybe) different flavors. They may pick up different vocabulary words that you don't use often. One of our kids recently picked up the word "decade" at a friend's home. And what parent can't smile when they hear their six-year-old proclaiming, "I haven't had a hot dog in a decade."

Another benefit for kids is that they feel more secure knowing that many adults care about their well-being. They feel at ease with their friends' parents and come to accept their corrections, kindness, and advice. A child who has been loved and cared for by a dozen or so neighborhood parents doesn't see strangers but friends. It's a good way to grow up.

And, of course, we come full circle back to the toys. There's really nothing like other people's toys and rediscovering some of your own toys too. Suddenly, that baby doll that has been at the bottom of the toy box for eight months becomes precious once more because it was loved by a visitor. We hope that your kids find co-op as satisfying and enriching as ours have. The friendships they form over graham crackers and milk can last a long time and bring much happiness to them.

Definition of a Babysitting Co-op Summary

A babysitting co-op is a formalized babysitting program consisting of parents who know and trust one another. These parents come together to provide their babysitting services for free in a systematic and structured way. Participating in a babysitting co-op creates a sense of freedom and support for parents, saves families money, eliminates the hassle of finding a sitter, offers socializing opportunities for children, and provides peace of mind for parents while they're away from their children.

CHAPTER 2
BASICS OF HOW TO CREATE A CO-OP

Creating a babysitting co-op is not only fun, but it's also easy to do. In this chapter, we are going to give you an overview of how to set up your own babysitting co-op in a step-by-step format. This brief overview will help you quickly determine if establishing a co-op is right for you and inform you about what is required. More detailed information can be found in the chapters that follow. It is important that you take some time to read the subsequent chapters as they will help you gain a greater understanding of each co-op principle.

Keep in mind that even though establishing your co-op does require a small investment of time in the early stages, the payoff is invaluable!

Step 1 – Identify Your Co-op Parents

The first and most important step in creating a co-op is to identify parents who are interested in participating. As mentioned earlier, these should be parents you know and trust. Inviting parents who live near you is always a good idea as well. This way nobody has to drive long distances for babysitting services.

Step 2 – Host an Informational Meeting

Once you've identified people who are interested, invite them to a meeting. At this meeting you can all sit down and talk about what a babysitting co-op entails and what benefits it will provide to everyone. It is important to provide your friends with a very clear understanding of what a co-op is and is not. Be sure to be very clear in sharing your vision of how this co-op will be established and function. Many parents have had experiences in trading babysitting time before, so they may come to this meeting with their own preconceived notions of how this co-op might function.

Step 3 – Identify a Co-op Leader

As with all formal activities and organizations, it's important to have someone in charge. Chances are good that you just might be the right person for the job since you've taken the time to learn more about babysitting co-ops.

The co-op leader is someone who enjoys being a leader and will act as the main contact for the group. The co-op leader (or leaders) will also most likely be the one who assembles and manages the tools that are needed to keep the co-op running smoothly. These tools include items such as the co-op tickets, co-op calendar, contact information sheet, and medical release forms, which are detailed later in the book. While it is not difficult to get these resources assembled, it is a necessary step in helping your co-op to run smoothly.

Step 4 – Host a Start-up Meeting

The goal of the start-up meeting is to establish yourselves as a formal co-op. With your co-op parents now in place, you'll want to set a date and time to meet and implement the program. In Chapter Eleven, you'll find a comprehensive agenda, which takes you through all the steps of hosting this meeting.

It is during this planning meeting that you'll iron out details such as setting up your co-op calendar. The co-op calendar tells everyone which babysitters are available on which days and at what times they'll be babysitting. You will also be learning how to use and exchange the co-op tickets, which act as your co-op currency. Finally, you'll need to establish your co-op rules and determine how to best communicate with one another.

Remind your parents to bring their own personal calendars with them so they can be sensitive to their individual and family commitments. Finally, it is during this meeting that you'll set up future planning meetings so babysitting shifts can be adjusted periodically. If you set these quarterly planning meetings in advance, you won't experience any gaps in your babysitting co-op program and you'll have continuous babysitting services available all year long.

Step 5 – Staying Connected

Babysitting co-ops allow both parents and children to build friendships with other people in their neighborhoods. We have made it a point to share with you some of our tried and tested ways of keeping these co-op connections strong. For instance, make it a point to enjoy a parent's only dessert night once a quarter. Another one of our favorite activities is to host a "wet and wild" water party for both co-op kids and parents.

Regularly scheduled social events (with and without the children) will help everyone to feel a sense of inclusion and unification. And it is at times like these when you'll really come to learn what is working for your co-op and where improvements can be made.

Basics of How to Create a Babysitting Co-op Summary

Creating a babysitting co-op is easy to do and involves inviting friends and acquaintances that you know and trust. This structured babysitting program eliminates those feelings of imposing on others and is designed to ensure a sense of equality when it comes to giving and spending your time. While a co-op does require an upfront investment of time, the benefits of saving money, having reliable care, and increasing friendships far outweigh this cost.

CHAPTER 3
THE ROLE OF THE CO-OP LEADER

The Role of the Co-op Leader

The babysitting co-op is a formal program which requires leadership, just like any other organization in our society. Successful co-op leaders understand the importance of being organized and are committed to their new venture. The babysitting co-op program requires proper leadership and needs to have someone acting as the head of the program. Let's explore this job a little further.

The role of the co-op leader is to represent the interests of all the co-op members and to keep the co-op group operating effectively. Being a co-op leader is quite a lot of fun and much easier than you'd imagine. In addition to having a great time with your friends, acting as the co-op leader also gives you a chance to shine. Typically we find that the co-op leader is a take-charge kind of person, a parent who enjoys coordinating events and getting people excited about new and innovative changes. The co-op leader's attitude greatly influences the tone for the entire group. In essence, you're like a cheerleader for the group. Your enthusiasm will be contagious and will set the stage for your group's experience.

While playing the role of "social coordinator" can be very satisfying, you'll take even more delight in seeing how babysitting co-op impacts the lives of your friends. Within a relatively short period of time, your friends will thank you for helping them find a way to enjoy reading a book that isn't found in the self-help or parenting section of the bookstore. They'll tell you how much fun it was to get the Christmas shopping done without worrying that their four-year-old might notice the remote controlled car hidden in the shopping cart. Regardless of what experience is shared, you'll have the pleasure of knowing that your initiatives and efforts have created something of significant value for others.

Now that we have a clearer picture as to the characteristics of a successful co-op leader, let's examine some additional aspects of the co-op leader's role. The co-op leader is the main point of contact for the co-op members. You will be the one to handle tasks such as orienting new members, replacing lost tickets, and ensuring that members are adhering to the co-op rules. Being a co-op leader does not mean that you have to do all the work. Rather, a good leader knows how to involve and motivate her team members, delegating tasks to other members and making sure things get done.

Get Everyone Involved

The co-op leader should invite parents to take on specific responsibilities to help reduce the workload. Most people are more than happy to accept a task or two and appreciate being acknowledged as a valuable part of the program. Don't be afraid to ask your co-op parents to lend a hand. Remember, people who actively contribute toward a joint cause take greater interest in the success of that cause and also feel a sense of ownership.

If you're feeling uncertain about your leadership abilities, invite a friend to join you in this role. There are several perks which come from having two leaders in place instead of just one. You will have a willing participant to help you accomplish the start-up process. This additional leader can also help you to maintain an objective view or generate some creative solutions when it's time to incorporate changes for the group. You can leave on vacation without worrying that a problem has arisen that will go unsolved until you get back. And finally, you'll have the moral support that's needed if a difficult situation arises within your co-op (i.e. resolving a conflict or having to ask a parent to leave the co-op).

Co-op Leader's Job Description

Here's a quick summary of the activities that fall under the direction of the co-op leader.

- Identify and invite co-op participants.
- Invite another friend to assist in leading the co-op group, if desired.
- Set a date and time for the start-up meeting which involves all co-op participants.
- At the initial start-up meeting, remind parents that you are here merely to facilitate the co-op. Everyone has a voice in how the babysitting co-op will function.
- Invite parents to assist in carrying out the following start-up activities:
  - ➢ Create a Contact List
  - ➢ Complete the master calendar
  - ➢ Outline the list of co-op rules
  - ➢ Design, duplicate, and laminate the co-op tickets
  - ➢ Obtain medical release forms
- Establish a completion date for the start-up tasks.
- Distribute completed start-up packets that include the above materials to co-op members once these packets have been assembled.
- Plan regular meeting times to evaluate how the program is functioning and for planning purposes.
- Ensure that all questions and concerns are resolved and that future issues are directed to her as well.
- Perform ongoing troubleshooting for the co-op when necessary.

Rotate the Co-op Leaders

After your co-op has been running for a year or so, you may find that you're ready to step down from your leadership position and hand this job off to another co-op member. The best way to ease into this transition is to share this decision with your co-op members a week or two prior to your next calendaring meeting. This way, no one will be taken by surprise or feel like they've been excluded when this conversation gets underway.

Communicating this news via e-mail is sufficient, or maybe you want to make this announcement a bit more personal and call each member on the phone. Regardless of how you choose to share the news, be sure that all the co-op members are in the loop prior to your upcoming meeting. Let your co-op friends know that the group is in need of a new leader and that this decision will be opened up for discussion at the calendaring meeting. This way, co-op members have time to evaluate whether or not they have the time and inclination to volunteer for the position.

Allowing other co-op members to participate in the role of co-op leader is a good way to enhance the dynamics already in place. We all have a lot to offer, and a new perspective may be just what your co-op needs to help it develop in new ways. Choosing a new leader does not have to be a formal event. Rather, it's best to invite co-op members who are interested in taking on this role to identify themselves at your next meeting and then finalize the decision as a group.

During the course of your leadership, you may have chosen to alter some of the guidelines suggested in this book. While making those subtle changes may have worked well for you, the new leaders will need to be familiar with how to handle unforeseeable events. Therefore, make sure you share adaptations and rules in depth with the new leader.

If this is a co-op parent's first time acting as a co-op leader, you may want to pair two of the willing candidates together. Inform the new leaders that they will work with you hand-in-hand to update and distribute any materials that may need to go out to the group. If you've been maintaining your co-op calendar, Contact List, and other materials electronically, offer to send them electronic copies of these documents. Additionally, let them know that you're available to assist them with any questions that might arise down the road. As new leaders, they will take great comfort in knowing that you are an available resource.

While there isn't a specific timeline attached to the co-op leader's job, we've found that it's best to maintain the same leader/leaders for a minimum of one year and not to exceed two years. It takes a while for new leaders to find their own comfort level. Co-op members need to be patient and give these new leaders some room to grow and develop their own leadership styles. One day, it just might be their turn to act as the co-op leader. And when that time comes, it will be comforting to know they have the support and understanding of the other co-op members they are now leading.

How to Become a Co-op Leader Summary

Remember that the primary goal of the co-op leader is to represent the interests of each member of the group. The co-op leader should set an enthusiastic tone for the group and is the one who will address issues should they arise. When acting as the co-op leader, invite other co-op members to assist in handling tasks as this will create a feeling of ownership for them as well. Additionally, be mindful that you do not need to fill this position indefinitely. You'll know when the time is right to hand this job on to another co-op parent.

CHAPTER 4
THE TICKETS

When parents hear about babysitting co-ops, the first questions asked are, "How am I compensated for my time?" and "How do I know that I'll be compensated in a fair way?" These are very good questions, and the answers are simple.

The babysitting co-op program operates on the exchange of tickets instead of cash. However, just like money, these tickets hold significant value because they represent time. When it's your co-op day and you're providing babysitting services, you'll earn tickets that you'll then be able to turn around and spend.

Tickets are broken up into one hour and half hour quantities. A predetermined number of tickets are provided to each co-op member when the program is initially organized. The amount of tickets each parent receives is based on the number of his or her participating children. Every parent starts with a total of eight hours of babysitting tickets per child.

The amount of tickets co-op members pay when picking up their children is one ticket per child per hour or half-hour for the time provided. Each member will initially start off with six one-hour tickets and four half-hour tickets, as shown on page 22. An additional copy of the Ticket Template can be found in the back of the book in Chapter Fourteen.

Let's look at a few examples to more fully understand how start-up tickets are distributed.

Start-Up Tickets
1 child x 8 hours per child = 8 hours of tickets
(6 one-hour tickets and 4 half-hour tickets)

2 children x 8 hours per child = 16 hours of tickets
(12 one-hour tickets and 8 half-hour tickets)

3 children x 8 hours per child = 24 hours of tickets
(18 one-hour tickets and 12 half-hour tickets)

You'll notice that a parent with only one child receives eight hours of tickets while a parent with three children receives 24 hours of tickets. While this might appear to be unfair, do not let this deceive you too quickly. As a general practice, we recommend that there shouldn't be more than six children present during any given babysitting shift. This number should include the babysitter's children as well.

The reason that the parent with one child has been given only eight hours worth of tickets is because she has greater earning potential. This mom can accept up to five more kids during her scheduled babysitting shift while the parent who has three children at home can only accept three additional children during her shift. Again, don't let this distribution ratio mislead you. The co-op member who has three children utilizing co-op services also has to pay out three times as many tickets as the parent of one child.

When Samantha went from paying for one child to paying for two, she noticed a huge difference in how quickly her co-op tickets were depleted. When she only had one child to pay for, she always felt like she had more than enough tickets at her disposal. However, when her second child started participating in co-op, maintaining a healthy stack of tickets became a bit more challenging. After spending a good deal of time talking with several different co-op groups, we've found that the vast majority felt that the ticket distribution system described above is the most fair, and that things seem to even themselves out in the end.

Let's look at a few examples to see how tickets are exchanged for co-op services. You can mix and match the tickets any way you like as long as the total number of tickets equals the total amount of time that was provided for your children.

Payment of Tickets
1 child x 3 hours = 3 tickets
(3 one-hour tickets or 2 one-hour tickets and 2 half-hour tickets)

1 child x 2.5 hours = 2.5 ticket
(2 one-hour tickets and 1 half-hour ticket)

3 children x 3 hours = 9 tickets
(9 one-hour tickets or 7 one hour tickets and 4 half-hour tickets)

3 children x 2.5 hours = 7.5 tickets
(7 one-hour tickets and 1 half-hour ticket)

Once the payment method has been explained to co-op members, we suggest that you make it a point to role play a couple of scenarios at your initial planning meeting. The exchanging of tickets may feel awkward at first, but it becomes second nature in no time at all. Role playing helps reinforce the payment method and demonstrates the fairness of the method to all of your co-op members.

Creating durable tickets from the beginning will save you a lot of time and energy down the road. Laminating the tickets is the best way to keep them from getting damaged while they're in circulation. If you'd like to authenticate the initial tickets in some way, you might choose to use a unique stamp, paper punch or a number system on the original tickets. Remember, you don't need to have all the tickets prepared in advance of your initial planning meeting. We've provided you with a formal agenda at the end of this book to help you keep track of all of those start-up tasks. Additionally, it's important to give everyone a chance to contribute their time and efforts on behalf of the group. Allow your co-op members to take on some of the responsibilities. This will give them a greater sense of involvement and will also reduce the number of tasks for the co-op leader.

~~ **1 Hour Ticket** ~~~	~~~ **1 Hour Ticket** ~~~
~~ **1 Hour Ticket** ~~~	~~~ **1 Hour Ticket** ~~~
~~ **1 Hour Ticket** ~~~	~~~ **1 Hour Ticket** ~~~
~~ **1/2 Hour Ticket** ~~~	~~~ **1/2 Hour Ticket** ~~~
~~ **1/2 Hour Ticket** ~~~	~~~ **1/2 Hour Ticket** ~~~

Rounding Up Your Payment

When paying for babysitting time, it's always best for the parent who's using the babysitting service to keep track of her own time. The co-op member who is doing the babysitting will be busy welcoming and settling the little ones arriving for her shift. As you can imagine, it can be hard for her to remember the exact amount of time she's provided for your child once you return.

Additionally, remember to be generous when it's time to pay your co-op friends. For example, let's say that you left one child at co-op and were gone 2.25 hours. When it's time to pay, you'll then provide the babysitting provider 2.5 hours worth of tickets instead of 2 hours worth of tickets. Likewise, if you left three kids for 3.25 hours, you'll need to round up your payment to 10 hours worth of tickets since it isn't possible to pay the babysitting parent with 9.75 hours in tickets.

Examples of Rounding Up

1 child x 2.25 hours = 2.5 tickets
(2 one-hour tickets and 1 half-hour ticket)

3 children x 3.25 hours = 10 tickets
(10 one-hour tickets or any combination that equals this total)

Chances are good that your co-op friend has probably provided a few snacks for your child while you were away and that she worked hard to make the activities enjoyable. Staying on good terms with another co-op parent is certainly more valuable than keeping that extra half hour ticket to yourself. This principle should be practiced whether you're paying for one, two or three children. If it's been a while since you've practiced multiplying decimals, then keep a calculator handy so your babysitter doesn't receive the short end of the stick.

Replacing Lost Co-op Tickets

Even the most organized parent has days when everything just seems to go wrong. You're late getting out the door, your two-year-old refuses to take her tutu off even though it is December, and maybe you'd really like to just jump back in bed and pull the blankets over your head. We can all relate. And this is why it's important for your co-op group to have plan for when valuable co-op tickets get lost or tossed in the laundry.

The babysitting co-op program is one that's based on honesty and respect, and it's important to give your friends the benefit of the doubt when they're requesting another set of co-op tickets. Often times, co-op tickets can become misplaced. It's even possible that a three-year-old decided to use them in an art project. Crazier things have been known to happen. Should a parent lose these tickets, she simply needs to approach the co-op leader and obtain a new set of replacement tickets equaling the amount she believes were lost. The parent who lost the tickets pays for the expenses of printing and laminating the new set of tickets. Again, it's important to discuss your replacement plan with your group to ensure that it meets everyone's approval.

Returning Your Co-op Tickets

Wouldn't it be nice if life could remain constant and unchanging every now and then? Kids wouldn't grow up so quickly, employment would remain steady, and good friends would always be just across the street to lend you an egg when you run out in the middle of making pancakes. However, life moves forward and change is constant, whether we like it or not.

Families move away because of better job opportunities, and new friends take their places. Children grow up and become more independent while new babies are born. Therefore, co-op members need to be aware of upcoming changes and plan accordingly. Your co-op group is bound to change with time, and you'll want to know how to handle these upcoming changes as they occur.

When parents no longer need the babysitting co-op, they need to start accumulating tickets to return to the co-op leader. They need to return the original amount of tickets they were given when they joined the program. So, if I joined the program with two children and was given 16 hours worth of time, I'd need to accumulate 16 hours worth of tickets. I would then turn them back in to the co-op leader before leaving the program.

Some parents might think that having to return tickets is unfair. They may feel like they should be able to spend out all of their remaining tickets because they've been an active and reliable part of the program. While this may be true, it is important to remember that when you first joined the group, your co-op tickets were given to you as a free gift of time. You did not have to earn those original hours; rather, the tickets were there to help you get started with a positive account balance.

There are other reasons why returning tickets is an important practice for your co-op group. If parents were to always spend out their remaining tickets, the co-op leader would constantly be creating new tickets for that new mom or dad who's filling a vacant position. Reproducing tickets can become expensive and can also consume excess time and energy. Additionally, if too many tickets are out in circulation, then the supply is going to exceed the demand, and the co-op could become unbalanced. Fortunately, we've never met a parent who's had a problem returning those initial tickets. Rather, the individual who is leaving the area is more often than not saddened by the thought of leaving this wonderful program behind.

When a parent is preparing to move away from your community, coming together for one more social event may be just what she needs to remind her that terrific people are scattered throughout the world. In no time at all, she'll have made a new circle of friends and will want to get her own co-op program up and running once again.

Take it from a real co-op mom who understands the importance of having the right information at her fingertips. When Angie was getting ready to leave her existing program she told us, "I was nervous about starting my own babysitting co-op group in my new neighborhood. However, my current co-op friends knew how to give me that vote of confidence. They all took some time to write valuable tips and funny co-op stories inside a new copy of *Babysitting Co-Op 101*. This going-away present was just what I needed to help me realize that soon I would have new friends to welcome into my own new co-op group."

Co-op parents understand the importance of supporting one another, staying connected, and creating a strong program to share with friends who come and go throughout the years. Staying connected is an important part in creating a fun and successful co-op. Several of the parents who contributed to our book told us how important it was to have some type of a treasury fund in place for get-togethers. We'll take a better look at how to strengthen our co-op connections in Chapter Nine.

Keep Those Tickets Moving

Finally, please remember that the co-op program cannot function properly if tickets are not being funneled through the system. That secret formula of circulation is also the secret formula to your babysitting quandary. And while it's always comforting to have a large number of tickets at your beck and call, it may not be in the best interest of the group.

Certainly, there are times when you might be saving up tickets for a future event, like attending a two-day conference or taking an extended vacation by yourself. We're always in favor of mini-vacations and if you need someone to carry your bags, just give us a call! In those cases, accumulating a large quantity of tickets is okay because those tickets will be sent right back into circulation within a short time. However, if you're holding on to too many tickets, the other co-op parents will quickly start feeling the crunch and it may become the topic of conversation at their next play date.

Finding ways to spend those "extra" tickets shouldn't be too hard. Plan an afternoon to repaint your bedroom or finish a project you've been putting off. Anyone who's ever tried to get some real remodeling done with little ones underfoot can appreciate just how challenging this can be. You get the idea. We want to ensure that everyone is happy and has plenty of opportunities to earn and use those priceless tickets.

Understanding the Co-op Tickets Summary

Babysitting co-op operates on the exchange of tickets. Tickets are traded amongst the group as the form of currency. Each parent receives eight hours of time per participating child. These start-up tickets help everyone begin with a positive balance and are divided into half-hour and one-hour denominations. Each parent will not be given the same amount of tickets because of their differing number of children; however, this method is fair and well-grounded. As parents begin to use the system they'll quickly discover that this system is quite fair to all involved. Always round up your payment when your payment does not end in a half hour or full hour segment. When rotating out of the co-op, return the same number of tickets that you originally received. Remember, the tickets were a free gift of time and need to be returned so they can be given to new parents joining the group. Finally, the key to a successful co-op is to keep the tickets moving. This program operates on supply and demand. A steady rotation of tickets and babysitting services will ensure that everyone has the same opportunity to earn and spend co-op tickets.

CHAPTER 5
THE CALENDAR

The co-op calendar is one of the most important tools for keeping your co-op organized and running smoothly. It plays an important role in the babysitting co-op because it enables parents to set appointments months in advance. You might ask, "Is it really possible for me to commit to an appointment two months down the road?" Yes, it's possible. In the past, you've never made this kind of commitment because you couldn't be sure you'd have a sitter lined up. Now, thanks to babysitting co-op, you'll always have the opportunity to commit to upcoming events because of the calendaring system.

For some people, it can feel intimidating to make commitments so far ahead. However, once the co-op schedule becomes second nature, you won't need to hesitate when a salon receptionist asks you how a Tuesday appointment might work. You'll automatically know that on Tuesdays it's your turn to babysit, so you'd better ask for a Wednesday morning instead. Because of this unique calendaring method, you have the comfort of knowing that someone else is scheduled for Wednesdays and can take your children while you're at the salon.

In this chapter, you'll learn all the secrets of how to set up and effectively use your babysitting co-op calendar.

Identifying a Shift

When the babysitting co-op meets for the first time, the leader (or another volunteer) will ask parents to arrive at the meeting with a "shift preference" in mind. A shift is defined by a specific day of the week and a specific time of day when you'll consistently be available to provide babysitting services. It's always good to have a second shift preference in mind just in case another parent is hoping to secure that same shift. Remember to look ahead to ensure that you won't have any personal commitments that may interfere with your designated shift.

With the meeting underway, the leader invites the parents to identify their preferred shifts. This means they need to identify both the day and the time period they want to claim as their babysitting shift. The leader will note these designated shifts on a master calendar, a white board, or a poster board. Using a larger writing surface can be handy because it allows all the co-op members to view the shifts as they're falling into place. These shifts are then projected three to four months out in advance and will remain in place until your co-op comes together for another planning session. The beauty of this practice is that it guarantees future babysitting services to all the co-op members for an extended period of time.

As your schedule takes shape, make a note of any holidays, school breaks, planned vacations or special events and block these times off the calendar. It's nice to have a school calendar with you at the meeting as well. If you do have a planned vacation that falls when you're scheduled to babysit, try and switch that particular day and time with another co-op member. If you're unable to make other arrangements, simply mark that particular shift as "unavailable," so other co-op members can plan accordingly.

Calendaring Throughout the Year

Planning meetings should be held three to four times each year so members can meet together and change their shifts based upon their changing family schedules. Using natural breaking points throughout the year for planning purposes seems to be most convenient. Calendaring segments may look something like this: January – May, June – August, September – December. Determine as a group how often you want to hold your planning meetings throughout the year.

A great way to ensure you don't have any down time with your calendar is to plan your next calendaring date when you're all together at that very first meeting. For example, when your group meets in the beginning of January to schedule the calendar for the following months (January, February, March, April, and May), select a date in mid to late

May for the next planning meeting. You'll find two main benefits come from advanced scheduling.

1.   More often than not, members won't have any commitments on their calendar that far ahead. This allows them to keep that date reserved just for co-op.

2.   If you take care of setting a date for the next calendaring segment in advance, you won't experience any gaps in the program. Babysitting shifts will be available continuously throughout the year.

The example below shows how a large babysitting co-op group might organize their shifts during a two-week period. These two weeks would then be repeated throughout the upcoming months to reflect a completed calendaring segment. You'll notice that the larger babysitting co-op consists of a total of 14 parents – starting with Stephanie and ending with Melinda. The larger co-op is represented by both Week 1 and Week 2. If your co-op is starting with a smaller number of parents, you'd repeat only the outlined shifts in Week1 for the upcoming months. The smaller co-op group includes only seven parents – starting with Stephanie and ending with Angie.

Sample White Board Demonstration – Week 1

	Mon	Tues	Wed	Thurs	Fri	Sat
a.m. 9-1	Stephanie	Traci	Rachel		Angie	
p.m. 12-4	Nicole	Jeff		Samantha		

Sample White Board Demonstration – Week 2

	Mon	Tues	Wed	Thurs	Fri	Sat
a.m. 9-1	Max	Kathy	Janet		Melinda	
p.m. 12-4	Paige	Sadie		Susan		

Assembling the Calendar

To get a master calendar put together, each parent needs to claim a day for his or her babysitting shift for the entire calendaring period. The simplest way to do this is to print out a calendar and pass it around to all the parents. The parents then pencil in the dates they're available to babysit, and you'll have a comprehensive shift calendar. One problem with this method is that it's time-consuming. You can spend a good chunk of the initial planning meeting just waiting around for your turn to write on the calendar. Luckily, we've come up with a more efficient method.

Instead of having just one calendar for everyone to write on, print enough calendars so you have one for each day of the co-op week. If your co-op will operate Monday through Thursday, print out four calendars, and write the days of the week (Monday, Tuesday, Wednesday, and Thursday) in large letters at the top of each calendar. The benefit to having several copies of blank calendars is that it helps to speed up the calendaring process. The Tuesday parents don't have to wait on the Monday parents to fill in their shifts for the upcoming months and so forth.

Next, divide the parents by the days of the week. If you have four parents taking Monday shifts, give them the calendar set labeled as "Monday Shifts" and let them work out which Mondays they'll each take. Together, they can fill out the entire Monday calendar, dividing up the Mondays with their available times. All they need to do is put their names and shifts on the calendar dates. See page 36 for a more visual example of how to do this. Parents should keep personal commitments in mind while they schedule their shifts. For instance, if one of their children's birthdays falls on a Monday, they'll probably want to defer to one of the other Monday parents for that particular day. Even though our examples show a set pattern for the co-op members, sometimes parents need to make adjustments and should have the adjustments reflected on the calendar.

When each group of parents has filled out their calendar, the co-op leader can collect them and use them to make a master calendar that will be distributed to each member of the co-op. As you can see, this method saves a lot of time at the set-up meeting.

Again, assembling the calendar will take place during the planning meeting(s) after all the shifts have first been agreed upon by all the parents. Be sure to come prepared with your personal calendars so everyone can work around any conflicting dates such as birthdays, anniversaries, family vacations, and school breaks.

Parents who are participating in a weekend co-op should wait until the weekdays have been scheduled out and then come together to discuss the weekend shifts at a later time. The weekend parents will then work together to arrange a schedule that is agreeable and then note these shifts onto one of the hard copy calendars. Details for Weekend Co-op will be covered in Chapter Ten.

The 30-Minute Rule

As a group, it's good to establish a minimum notice time for babysitting shifts. Perhaps a 30-minute rule would work well. For instance, if your shift falls every Monday morning (from 9:00 a.m. – 1:00 p.m.), you would be obligated to be available for babysitting requests until 8:30 a.m. Monday morning. If no one has contacted you by this time (30 minutes prior to your shift) then you are no longer obligated to remain at home and fulfill the babysitting commitment. If a parent contacts you after 8:30 a.m., it is up to you to decide whether you'll take on that particular babysitting request.

A final word on scheduling: it's always good to call as far in advance as possible when securing babysitting time. Shifts are open on a "first come, first serve" basis, and available openings may get booked quickly. Remember that each caregiver may only care for six children at a time, including his or her own children. Additionally, it's important for those who are providing babysitting services to respond promptly. Parents are counting on your availability, and often times they'll want to confirm plans a few days in advance.

Electronic Calendaring Programs

Today, most computers and handheld devices are sold with a calendaring program already installed and ready to go. This is a huge benefit because when you put your calendar together, using an electronic calendar can save you quite a bit of time. Electronic calendaring programs allow you to schedule recurring events on a daily, weekly, bi-weekly or monthly basis, which takes care of a lot of the work for you. Additionally, you can easily transfer these electronic calendars via the internet and even post them, or their link, on a central webpage.

If you aren't interested in spending any money on a calendaring program, the same tasks can be accomplished in a relatively short period of time by writing each shift down on paper calendar or setting up a calendaring system in Microsoft Excel®.

Google Calendar can be a fantastic tool for handling babysitting co-op shifts. If most or all of the members of your co-op already use Google Calendar for their personal, professional, or community schedules, adding a calendar for babysitting co-op will work with what they already have in place. As the group leader, you could create a Google calendar with all of the babysitting shifts clearly marked. Once your calendar is finalized, click the down-arrow button next to the calendar and select "Share this Calendar." Then you enter the email addresses of the members of your co-op and click "Save." Once you click "Save," each person you shared the calendar with will receive an email invitation to view the calendar. They need to click on the link contained in the email to add the calendar to their own accounts.

Small vs. Large Co-op Groups

Smaller babysitting co-op groups tend to plan babysitting shifts that fall weekly for their members. If your co-op group is larger, you can plan to set your babysitting shifts to an every-other-week schedule. It's up to each group to determine shift times and durations. Again, individual schedules will play a large role in this part of the process. Several groups have found that a four-hour shift works well for both the parents and the children. Additionally, you'll see that with a larger co-op group, you're able to overlap each shift by one hour during the middle of the day. This overlap provides parents with the flexibility to meet mid-day commitments such as lunch dates. Adding a Friday or Saturday evening to your calendar is also an option that affords parents to take advantage of some free time together. This information will be covered in greater depth in Chapter Ten.

On page 34, you can see how a small babysitting co-op group decided to schedule alternate morning and afternoon shifts throughout the week and how they projected this information for the entire month. They also chose to include weekends as part of their babysitting co-op plan.

January		Small Group (5 Members) Co-op Calendar				
Sun	Mon	Tues	Wed	Thurs	Fri	Sat
		1 *Holiday Break No Co-op*	2 *Holiday Break No Co-op*	3 *Holiday Break No Co-op*	4 *Holiday Break No Co-op*	5 *Holiday Break No Co-op*
6	7 9-11 Jill	8 12-4 Traci	9 9-1 Diana	10 12-4 Paige	11 9-1 Samantha	12 *Jill
13	14 9-11 Jill	15 12-4 Traci	16 9-1 Diana	17 12-4 Paige	18 9-1 Samantha	19 *Traci
20	21 9-11 Jill	22 12-4 Traci	23 9-1 Diana	24 12-4 Paige	25 9-1 Samantha	26 *Diana
27	28 9-11 Jill	29 12-4 Traci	30 9-1 Diana	31 12-4 Paige	1 9-1 Samantha	2 *Paige

Weekend co-op members (Saturday evening shifts are set at the time of the request to provide flexibility for both parents).

With the larger babysitting co-op group, shown on page 36, the parents are able to rotate into an every-other-week schedule because of the number of participants. What does this mean for these parents? It means that they now have 52 hours of babysitting hours available to them simply because they were willing to commit to two babysitting shifts per month. This is just one of the really amazing benefits of this program! Additionally, they're also able to spread out their Saturday evening shifts over two months instead of one.

Take a moment to note how Stephanie and Nicole's shifts (e.g., Monday, January 7th) overlap by one hour and let's talk about why this is a benefit to your group. Often times the lunch hour can be a busy time of day when parents need a little more flexibility. The one hour overlap opens up a larger window of time for plans in the middle of the day. Scheduling two shifts within one day also allows parents to be away for longer periods of time when needed. Let's take a look at a specific example.

Traci works part-time as real estate agent. For Traci, the babysitting co-op is a perfect answer to her working schedule because of the flexibility it provides. However, every year Traci is required to participate in some additional training seminars to keep her license current. Having two shifts available on the calendar enables Traci to conveniently attend these trainings. You may be wondering how this is possible since Traci is away from the neighborhood and can't manage the transportation. Prior to her training, Traci would make it a point to schedule time with Stephanie and Nicole for Monday, January 7th. She would then arrange for either Stephanie to drop her son off to Nicole at the end of her shift which is 1:00 p.m. or for Nicole to pick her son up from Stephanie's home prior to the beginning of her shift which starts at 12:00 p.m. In exchange for this courtesy Traci would then offer to pay one of the mom's an extra half hour or one hour ticket. The amount of "bonus time" can be determined by the parties involved.

As you can see, this scenario is a win-win for everyone involved! Traci is able to attend her work training with peace of mind because she knows that her son is with adults that are caring and responsible. As for her son, he is having a good time playing with friends and is spending time in a friendly environment. The final benefit to this scenario is that Traci didn't have to pay a dime for this childcare arrangement! Her money stays right where it belongs, with her.

January   **Large Group (14 Members) Co-op Calendar**

Sun	Mon	Tues	Wed	Thurs	Fri	Sat
		1 *Holiday Break No Co-op*	2 *Holiday Break No Co-op*	3 *Holiday Break No Co-op*	4 *Holiday Break No Co-op*	5 *Holiday Break No Co-op*
6	7 9-1 Stephanie 12-4 Nicole	8 9-1 Traci 12-4 Jill	9 9-1 Angie	10 12-4 Melinda	11 9-1 Rachel	12 *Stephanie
13	14 9-1 Sharla 12-4 Paige	15 9-1 Michael 12-4 Sadie	16 9-1 Janet	17 12-4 Nick	18 9-1 Samantha	19 *Nicole
20	21 9-1 Stephanie 12-4 Nicole	22 9-1 Traci 12-4 Jill	23 9-1 Angie	24 12-4 Melinda	25 9-1 Rachel	26 *Traci
27	28 9-1 Sharla 12-4 Paige	29 9-1 Michael 12-4 Sadie	30 9-1 Janet	31 12-4 Nick	1 9-1 Samantha	2 *Jill

Weekend co-op members (Saturday evening shifts are set at the time of the request to provide flexibility for both parents).

Assess the Program

When your co-op group is in its starting stages, we recommend holding an assessment meeting a month or two into the first calendaring segment. The purpose of the assessment meeting is to make sure that everyone is implementing the program in the same manner. This also gives co-op parents an opportunity to ask any questions or raise any concerns that may have surfaced since the group first met. Taking the time to meet six to eight weeks into the program helps the group make any course corrections that are required. Be sure to set the date for the assessment meeting while you're still together at the initial start-up meeting. You'll want to ensure that everyone can be there.

Make the assessment meeting a fun event. It doesn't have to be overly formal or arduous. Turn this gathering into something that will also help to strengthen the bonds of friendship within your group. A possible suggestion is that everyone meets at a local restaurant for a late dinner or dessert, leaving your spouse, a relative, or a friend at home with the sleeping children. This informal get-together creates the perfect opportunity for co-op member to troubleshoot any concerns or potential problems. Later in Chapter Six, we will learn how one co-op parent (Tiffany) was able to troubleshoot a potentially difficult situation just by keeping the lines of communication open. As we all know, a little bit of foresight and early communication can go a long way in ensuring that everyone remains happy.

Now that your co-op has been operating for a few weeks, you'll find that parents will be eager to compare notes and funny stories about co-op and discuss how co-op is working in their lives. And don't be surprised if you learn something new about yourself. Children are notorious for being brutally honest. They love to share innocent yet possibly embarrassing facts about their parents. Once the desserts are served and some chatting is out of the way, keep the business part of your get-together short and simple. Staying connected as co-op members is vital to the success of your program. In Chapter Nine, we address why this is so important and have provided creative ways to accomplish this goal.

Calendaring for Co-op Summary

A successful babysitting co-op depends upon reliable members and a reliable calendaring system. While creating and following-up on the calendar is one of the co-op leader's responsibilities, other co-op members can be invited to fulfill this job. Good calendaring will ensure that the co-op runs smoothly.

To facilitate the calendaring meeting, prepare a large poster board or white board so everyone can see the calendar as shifts are chosen. Check the school calendar for holidays and breaks, and note them on the final calendar, which will be distributed after the planning meeting. Try to coordinate shift preferences so everyone gets a shift that works with their schedules. At the end of the meeting, schedule a date for an assessment meeting and the next planning meeting. The assessment meeting should fall 4-6 weeks after the initial planning meeting while the next calendaring meeting should be three to four months away. Ask everyone to review and approve the final calendar before distributing the final copy to the entire group.

CHAPTER 6
PRINCIPLES OF A SUCCESSFUL
BABYSITTING CO-OP

"Feelings of worth can flourish only in an atmosphere where individual differences are appreciated, mistakes are tolerated, communication is open, and rules are flexible...." Virginia Satir

How fun would life be if we all went around wearing the same hairstyles or decorating our homes in the same color schemes or with identical pieces of furniture? What if we had the habit of dining with friends every Friday night only to find that chicken cordon bleu was our only option? While these examples seem silly, we think it helps to point out the importance of valuing and appreciating our differences. Wouldn't you agree that often times it's these unique differences that we come to treasure most in others?

We all have extraordinary acquaintances, people we admire for their strength of character, their artistic abilities, or the way they say just the right thing when you're at a loss for words. As parents we're doing our best to raise our children and make a difference in the world. While we may not be helping to establish hospitals or invent the latest and greatest gadgets, we too, are extraordinary people. We strive to run respectful households, lift the spirits of others, and prepare our children for productive lives of their own.

As you're looking forward to babysitting co-op, it's essential to remember to embrace differences. Some may wonder if it's possible for a cohesive group to come together when people have different viewpoints, different talents, and different modes of operation. We would answer that not only can you come together, but in doing so, you'll find greater strength in your varied talents. Members of a cooperative group don't need to be the same in order to make it successful.

History is full of stories about people who have thrown their strengths together to create something bigger and better than what they could've done on their own. Consider the efforts of our Founding Fathers. These men (lawyers, merchants, and physicians to name a few) came together in behalf of countrymen near and far to secure our independence. Truly these heroic efforts required a tremendous amount of compromise and collaboration. Another example is the story of Susan B. Anthony. She devoted her life to promoting equal rights for women, working tirelessly to empower other women to claim their Constitutional right to vote. While we don't foresee the babysitting co-op making it into the history books, the principle of synergy and joint collaboration holds true for your own babysitting co-op program.

A successful babysitting co-op starts with a strong foundation. This foundation is built upon the Three C's: communication, customization, and courtesy. Will there be differences of opinion along the way? Of course. Try to see these differences positively rather than with judgment or criticism. You may just find that these various differences can send your group in a new direction, creating a better resource for all to enjoy.

While we encourage you to create a flexible program that meets your specific needs, keep in mind that some structure must exist in order for things to run smoothly. A strong co-op program would not last long without rules, so we've taken care of the guesswork for you. An outline of rules, which you'll want to review as a group, can be found in Chapter Seven and covers the following topics:

- Handling Meals
- Discipline
- Extending and Switching Shifts
- Tardiness
- Replacing Lost Tickets
- Number of Kids per Shift
- Adding New Members
- Handling Emergencies and
- Three Strikes Policy

These rules will act as the framework for your new foundation and will greatly reduce potential misunderstandings. Building a strong foundation means providing parents with a welcoming environment where everyone can communicate their concerns and desires. While your babysitting co-op will have one or two parents acting as the co-op leaders, the program really belongs to all of the co-op members. Customizing your babysitting co-op is another aspect that deserves time and consideration. And finally, bestowing the types of courtesies that you would expect to receive from others will ensure that your group gets started on the right foot. With this in mind, let's take a few moments to explore the "Three C's" in greater depth.

Communication

The babysitting co-op is a program that operates on the voluntary exchange of time and services. As noted above, it is essential that good communication exists among all the co-op members. Individuals are more likely to go the extra mile when they feel like they're valued and contributing members of a group. While someone ultimately has to open and lead the group, questions can be phrased in a warm and inviting manner. Asking open-ended questions ("How does everyone feel about using time-out as a disciplining technique?" or "How should we handle parents who are late picking up their children?") will create a sense of unity. As a result, co-op members will feel personally invested because someone thought enough to ask for their input.

As parents, we know that children tend to demonstrate more acceptance and support for family rules when they are involved in the planning of those family rules. Likewise, we all can appreciate how telling our children exactly how to do things can create an uninviting and challenging situation. Many times children will meet us with resistance, tantrums, sassiness or obstinacy simply because they feel we are imposing our will upon them rather than working with them. This principle of joint collaboration holds true for adults as well. Everyone has something of significance to contribute. Ultimately, the goal is to encourage the co-op members to find their voices and help establish the guidelines that will best fit your co-op so they will want to support and adhere to your guidelines. And as the old adage goes, "It's easier to catch more flies with honey than with vinegar."

Co-op members should feel that they can voice their opinions at any time whether it be via e-mail or in a joint forum during socials and/or planning meetings. It is important, however, to realize that while everyone may not agree with their ideas their input is a valuable and necessary part of the co-op culture. Group social activities will help co-op members to strengthen those bonds of friendship. Establishing a high level of open communication with regards to the co-op program and the children is essential and a great way to ensure long lasting satisfaction with the co-op program.

Customization

In life, we all have different needs and desires, and babysitting co-op is no different. When organizing your babysitting co-op, unique concerns and expectations will surface as you press forward in this journey. Members will move out of the neighborhood, and new parents will replace their vacant positions. Recognize that the needs and dynamics of your group will inevitably change and that minor adjustments must be made along the way.

While the information contained in this book provides you with everything you need to get your group off the ground, don't be afraid to stray from the guidelines. Establishing rules is necessary; however, it's best to approach these guidelines with some flexibility. Each group is going to operate differently, and it may take some trial and error to figure out what works best. The important thing to keep in mind is that everyone is coming together to satisfy the greater goals of the entire group.

Here is an example of how one co-op group took this principle and put it into action. Tiffany had found a number of parents who were eager to get their babysitting co-op program rolling. Everything went smoothly at first, and then, within a few weeks, Tiffany's group found that the afternoon co-op shifts were being underused. Most of the co-op members had very young children, so these moms were all trying to schedule their appointments and run their errands during the morning hours. Filling up a morning shift was never a problem. In fact, there was often too much demand for these morning hours. Upon closer examination, Tiffany discovered that her group valued having their children nap in their own homes during the afternoons and didn't want them to be out at this time of day.

It was easy to see that the afternoon shifts really served no purpose for her co-op members. And yet the moms that had chosen these afternoon babysitting shifts still needed to earn and accumulate co-op tickets. Tiffany quickly brought this observation to light and made the necessary adjustments to resolve what could have been a perpetual problem. The answer the group implemented was brilliant. Tiffany's co-op decided to schedule two morning shifts that ran simultaneously and drop their afternoon babysitting shifts altogether.

Customizing their babysitting shifts was the solution they needed to ensure that their program continued to run smoothly. In the end, the moms were happier because this solution not only met their needs, but it also met the needs of their children. Remember that customization is one of the keys to a successful co-op experience.

Courtesy

Every co-op member needs to feel that their time and efforts are appreciated. And while we may be in a rush to get to our appointments on time or meet an old friend for lunch, we should not forget the value of extending common courtesies to one another. Here are a few courtesy points to keep in mind that will aid in strengthening that solid foundation which we discussed earlier.

- Take a few minutes to show genuine interest and concern for the well-being of your co-op members.
- Be punctual when dropping off and picking up your children.
- Honor the established rules for payment, switching shifts, and other aspects of your babysitting co-op program.
- Be quick to recognize and praise the good behavior that your co-op kids may have displayed while in your care. (Parents always want to know if their children are practicing the social skills they're teaching at home).
- Likewise, be sure to inform a parent of any disruptive behavior displayed while their children were in your care.
- Share any unusual circumstances your child might be experiencing when you drop your child off for another member's care (sensitivity due to an ear infection, teething discomforts, unusual lethargy, etc.).
- Give the children in your care the time and attention they deserve.
- Be aware of the number of tickets you've accrued and have left to spend. (Saving up tickets for a special event is fine, but the majority of the tickets need to be in circulation in order for the

program to function well).
- Make babysitting co-op a fun experience for everyone involved!

Putting these principles into practice will serve you well throughout the years. Remember that in addition to providing a wonderful service to one another, you're also in the business of building relationships that will grow and become an irreplaceable part of your parenting experience.

Principles of a Successful Babysitting Co-op Summary

Recognize that your co-op members will come into the program with different needs and expectations. Use effective communication techniques (such as open ended questions) to help members embrace new ideas and create a quality program. Acknowledge the value of the suggestions that are shared and give thoughtful consideration to implementing these ideas when possible. Discuss the "Three C's" with your group and remind co-op members that future insights can be either shared directly with the co-op leader or presented to the group as a whole, via e-mail, or at social and/or planning events.

CHAPTER 7
ESTABLISHING RULES FOR BABYSITTERS

Not too long ago, Samantha sat down to play a game of *Candy Land* with her two daughters, Sydney, age five, and Mia, age three. Samantha thought this would be a great way to spend the afternoon with her girls and expected everyone to have a great time. The game board was neatly placed on the table and the cards were shuffled and stacked high. The girls took great care in determining whether they wanted a green, blue, or red gingerbread man to play with. Samantha took the leftover token, and all the gingerbread men were happily placed on board.

Within a matter of minutes, this cheerful event soon resembled a dark, threatening storm just waiting to break loose. Mia did not want to wait her turn and insisted on going twice in a row. Sydney reluctantly allowed her to go again because of Samantha's motherly stare which told her to be patient with her sister. Now it was finally time for Sydney to draw a card. As soon as she lifted the card from the stack, Mia's tiny hand snatched Sydney's gingerbread man and scooted it up the board to Lord Licorice's Castle. Samantha, feeling a bit flustered, hadn't given up hope, yet.

Sydney had been a good sport up until now; however, she was quickly becoming annoyed and couldn't understand why Mia just couldn't follow the rules. Still hoping to revive this bonding opportunity, Samantha took a moment to let Mia know that she needed to wait her turn so everyone had a chance to play. When Mia's turn came around once again, things did not improve. Mia decided to preview the playing cards and excitedly spread them out all over the board. Sydney broke down into sobs, declaring, "Mia always ruins the game! It's all her fault," and, "Why do I have to have a sister anyway?"

How was it that such a simple activity like playing a board game had turned into such a mess? Why was it that Samantha's good intentions had resulted in sheer frustration for all involved? Clearly, it was because there was a lack of understanding amongst all the players. Sydney, being older and somewhat wiser, had learned the rules of *Candy Land* and knew what to expect. Mia, on the other hand, was inexperienced and uninformed. In her mind, she had her own set of rules for this game and was equally frustrated because she wasn't being allowed to play the game her way. All of this could have been prevented if Samantha had taken the time to clarify the rules and ensure that both Sydney and Mia knew what was expected of them as players.

Having a formal set of rules in place for your co-op is essential. Establishing clear rules at the very beginning will help to eliminate misunderstandings about how the program operates. Additionally, discussing what's expected from all the parents will ensure that no one feels taken advantage of and that everyone is treated fairly. The co-op leader should go over the rules listed below and then open this part of the planning meeting up for discussion. Keep in mind that the real objective is to outline a set of rules that meets the needs of all the co-op members. Encourage the co-op members to speak openly about how they feel about certain rules. One co-op member may feel that running 10 minutes beyond their appointed pick-up time is not a huge infraction while another co-op member may feel that being even 10 minutes late is not acceptable.

Listed below are a set of suggested rules that moms have found to be most useful. Invite a co-op member, or the alternate leader, to take notes during this portion of the planning meeting so nothing is overlooked. These rules not only provide you with a firm guideline to follow but also a way of compensating for rules that might be broken. Remember to be flexible and alter the rules as needed for your particular co-op. Following the meeting, be sure to note the rules in written form and include these rules with your start-up materials.

Suggested Co-op Rules

Meals
A parent can either bring a packed meal or ask the babysitter to provide a meal for the child. If the babysitter provides a meal for the child, then the parent owes the babysitter an extra half-hour ticket in addition to the normal amount of tickets for each child that is fed. Here is an example of how the tickets are dispersed when a meal is provided for two children.

2 children x 2 hours + a meal = 5 hours of tickets
(4 hour tickets for babysitting time and 2 half-hour tickets for lunch)

Discipline
This subject should be approached with great sensitivity and plenty of open communication. Many parents have strong feelings about what is and is not appropriate. It is important that the group discuss this matter at length to find a method that is agreeable to everyone.

The disciplining method that has worked well for most groups is time-out. If a child is misbehaving and causing grief for the babysitter or other children, then the child is taken to a specific time-out spot or chair. The child is asked to remain there until their behavior is under control. If the behavior does not improve, then the babysitter has the right to contact the parent and ask them to please return from their activity to pick up their child. Once the time-out has been completed, remember to welcome the child back into the playing environment with words of kindness and comfort.

Extending Shift Hours
Co-op members are usually happy to accommodate a request to bring a child 15 minutes early or 15 minutes following the end of their shift. If you need additional time outside the scheduled shift, you should contact the babysitter directly to see if arrangements can be made. Be mindful that while the sitter may be able to help you out, she is not obligated to babysit longer than her scheduled shift. At the initial planning meeting, the leader should remind co-op members that we all keep very busy schedules, and you may be told "no" simply because that particular babysitting parent has other obligations to meet either right before or immediately following her shift. Requesting an extension for babysitting time should be handled between the direct

parties and does not need to involve the co-op leader.

Switching Shifts

In the real world, we are not always able to honor our commitments. Children get sick, family comes to visit and, frankly, sometimes we just have a bad day and can't handle the thought of caring for additional children. If you need to switch your scheduled shift, call one of your co-op friends and ask them if they can trade shifts with you. It is your responsibility to find a substitute and then communicate this change to the remaining co-op members. As a courtesy, you'll want to notify the rest of the group as soon as possible.

If you're unable to find a replacement and you cannot adjust your schedule and truly need to cancel your shift, then be sure to communicate these unusual circumstances to the other parents. Again, be prompt in notifying your co-op friends about this cancellation. They may have commitments already in place for that particular day and timeframe. Pulling a shift from the calendar needs to be treated as a last resort.

Tardiness

Once in a while, parents run late in returning to a babysitter's home and their tardiness is truly unintentional. However, as we all know, some parents tend to run late regardless of what they're doing or where they're going. As a group, you need to decide what determines tardiness. Is a parent considered late if she doesn't meet the exact time she noted when scheduling her time, or is she considered tardy if she arrives after the end of a specific shift? Here are two hypothetical examples to consider when establishing your guidelines.

> **Example A - Arriving Late During A Shift**
> It's Thursday evening and Julie calls Melissa to see if her two children can come over for co-op the following morning. Melissa is scheduled for Friday mornings from 9:00 a.m. to 1:00 p.m. and says that she's happy to put the kids on her calendar. The following morning, Julie arrives at Melissa's home at 9:00 a.m. and tells Melissa that she'll be back at 10:30 a.m. The appointed time comes and Julie has not yet returned to Melissa's house. Time is ticking by and finally at 11:00 a.m. Julie arrives at Melissa's door, pays Melissa four hours' worth of tickets, and thanks Melissa for her time.

➤ **Example B - Arriving Late At The End Of A Shift**
Once again, it's Thursday evening and Julie calls Melissa to see
if her two children can come over for co-op the following
morning. Melissa is scheduled for Friday mornings from 9:00
a.m. to 1:00 p.m. and says that she's happy to put the kids on
her calendar. The following morning, Julie arrives at Melissa's
home at 9:00 a.m. and tells Melissa that she'll be back at 1:00
p.m., which is the end of the co-op shift. The appointed time
comes and Julie has not yet returned to Melissa's house. Time is
ticking by and soon Melissa notices that it's now 1:15 p.m.
Melissa has a doctor's appointment for her own toddler at 1:30
p.m. and is now starting to feel the pressure of her time
constraints.

Julie arrives at 1:20 p.m., apologizes for running late, and thanks
Melissa for her time. Melissa receives nine hours' worth of tickets
because Julie has made it a point to rounded up her payment since
she's almost reached 4.5 hours

(2 kids x 4.5 hours = 9 hours' worth of tickets). Once Julie is out the
door, Melissa frantically grabs her purse and the diaper bag and dashes
off to the doctor's office.

As you can see, taking the time to discuss punctuality up front will
greatly reduce the likelihood of having this conversation later down
the road. Co-op members need to be considerate of one another's
schedules. Making it a point to be punctual is just a common courtesy.
Additionally, being on time will prevent any hard feeling from
developing between co-op members.

How you choose to identify tardiness is up to the group. Is a parent
tardy if they return 10-15 minutes after their designated time as noted
in Example A? Or will you only consider a parent tardy if they arrive
after the shift time has ended as in Example B? Once you've chosen a
way in which to identify tardiness, it's important to determine how
much time can pass by before a parent is considered officially late.
When a parent exceeds the tardiness limit (as determined by your
group), she is required to pay the babysitting co-op member a one-
hour ticket per child for her tardiness. Let's take another look at how
Julie and Melissa would handle Julie's late arrival.

Paying Penalty Tickets for Tardiness

Julie arrives at Melissa's home at 9:00 a.m. and tells Melissa that she'll be back at 1:00 p.m. The appointed time comes and Julie has not yet returned to Melissa's house. Time is ticking by, and soon Melissa notices that it's now 1:15 p.m. Melissa has a doctor's appointment for her own toddler at 1:30 p.m. and is now starting to feel the pressure of her time constraints.

Julie arrives at 1:20 p.m., apologizes for running late and thanks Melissa for her time. Here is how Melissa would be compensated given Julie's tardiness.

2 kids x 4.5 hours = 9 hours' worth of tickets
2 kids x 1 hour for tardiness = 2 hours' worth of tickets
Total Amount Paid = 11 hours' worth of tickets

While we want to be understanding of reasonable delays, we also want to encourage promptness. Having a one-hour ticket penalty rule creates a strong incentive for parents to be on time.

If a co-op member notices a tardiness pattern occurring with a certain parent, she has the right to share these incidents with the co-op leader. In fact, she should make it a point to bring these infractions to the co-op leader's attention because she is probably not the only one affected. In a few moments, we'll discuss how repeated offenses should be handled in the Three Strikes segment of this chapter.

Replacing Tickets

Let me start by saying that in our 10 plus years of co-op we have rarely had to replace a set of tickets for our co-op members. Nor have we ever had to provide that same member with a second set of replacement tickets. Thank goodness this is a rare problem. However, take comfort in knowing that if this problem arises, we do have a solution for you.

As a babysitting co-op group, you'll want to have a backup plan in place for members who misplace their tickets or accidentally toss them in with the laundry. The most common solution to this problem is to allow members to have one complimentary replacement set equaling the amount they believe to be lost. Once this discovery is made, the co-op member notifies the co-op leader and should be prepared to cover any expenses which may come about by reproducing another set of tickets. The co-op leader may also invite this member to handle the actual reproduction of these tickets as well.

If a second set of tickets needs to be provided to the same co-op member, it will be her responsibility to earn them back from the co-op leader. This second set of replacement tickets will not be given to the parent as a courtesy. Let's say that the co-op parent believes she lost around 10 hours' worth of tickets, yet again. The co-op member then must provide 10 hours' worth of babysitting to the group without receiving payment directly from the other co-op participants. Once the hours are completed, then the co-op leader will provide her with the replacement tickets, which are reproduced at her expense.

Number of Participating Children
As parents, we want to ensure that each child within our care receives the time and attention he or she deserves. With this in mind, it is important to limit the number of children within your care during your babysitting shift. Many groups have found that having a total number of six kids at one time is a manageable number. This number should also include your own children. Therefore, if two of your children are at home full time, you would then be able to accept four more kids during your shift. Because infants (babies under 12 months) require so much extra attention, it is a good idea to limit the number of infants within each babysitting shift to one.

Do not feel as if you need to hold fast to the recommended amount of six children per shift. Some groups have left the decision of how many children to schedule strictly up to the mom who's providing the babysitting services. If your group tends to have a number of young children, you may feel that attending to four kids is sufficient. However, if your group is made of up of older children who play well together and entertain themselves, then feel free to go beyond the recommended number of six, within reason. Here again, this rule is completely subjective to the specific needs of your group.

Adding New Members
Members come and go as personal circumstances change. Families move, and word of the babysitting co-op spreads among other parents and friends. It should be up to the entire babysitting co-op group to determine when new members are allowed to join the program and how the screening process should work. Is allowing a new parent to join mid-session agreeable? Does everyone need to know the new parent and their children prior to joining? Or is having a solid

recommendation from one or two of the existing members sufficient?

Here are some factors to consider in making this decision. Does the co-op need additional babysitting shifts? Can a new member join in the middle of a calendar term or does she need to wait until the next calendaring segment starts? If you allow someone to join in the middle of a calendaring segment, is the co-op leader willing to update and distribute a new calendar, contact information, medical form, and tickets? Will the new parent agree to the already established rules? Covering these points in advance will help to eliminate potential conflict at a later time. We highly recommend that you clarify this decision at your initial planning meeting and ensure that everyone is comfortable with the process.

Realistically, adding new members at the beginning of a new calendaring segment works best. It is strongly recommended that an informal orientation meeting is held 30 minutes prior to your normally scheduled meeting time with the new parent who'll be joining the group. You might want to invite the parent who's recommended this new member to sit in on the orientation, creating a greater sense of comfort for the new member.

Conducting an informal sit down such as this will give you a chance to cover the finer points of the co-op program. Additionally, this casual setting will provide just the right opportunities for the new member to address any unanswered questions in a comfortable forum. An easy way to orient new co-op members is by following your start-up agenda found on page 99. This agenda will help you cover all the information that a new member needs to know. At the end of the orientation, your new co-op member will know all the ins and outs and will be ready to jump in with the rest of the group. One final note: be sure to let this new parent know that she is not obligated to participate. If the parent decides that co-op isn't for her, give her a comfortable way out. She then can thank the co-op leader for her time and excuse herself prior to the rest of the meeting getting underway.

Emergency Contact
While we never anticipate an emergency occurring during your co-op shift, it's always better to be safe than sorry. The Contact List, which is found in Chapter Fourteen, should always be kept up-to-date. If you are not going to be reachable through your normal means (i.e. your home number or a cell phone number), be sure to leave a name and a

phone number for the babysitter to use in case of an emergency. And, as a courtesy, be sure to let your emergency contact know ahead of time that you've shared their name and phone number as a backup for the babysitting co-op group.

Medical Emergencies

In the many years that co-op has existed, we've never had an incident where medical attention has been required, and this has brought us a lot of comfort. Unfortunately, however, even the most vigilant parent can't be present with her child, or the co-op children, every moment of every day. If an incident occurs that requires immediate attention, be sure to act quickly and use sound judgment for the interest of the child. Of course, it's always best to try and reach the child's parents (or emergency contact) when the emergency is taking place. However, if you don't have time to reach the parents because of the severity of the situation, remain calm, and take action.

A standard Medical Release form needs to be provided to and completed by each participating co-op member. These forms should be completed and turned in at the initial planning meeting. Once all the materials are in place, the medical form will be distributed along with each member's start up folder. In fact, a parent who is delinquent in returning or completing his or her form should not be providing or receiving babysitting services until this task is accomplished. You just don't want to take the risk of being the one parent who finds herself with an injured child and inadequate information.

Completing this form is a painless process when you consider the difficulties you may encounter when trying to receive unauthorized emergency medical care for a child other than your own (See page 104 for a reproducible form). Remember to keep these forms in a convenient location, where they can be easily accessed if needed. Additionally, these forms should be updated on a regular basis so the information remains current. When it comes time for you to rotate out of babysitting co-op, return all the forms of the other participating parents to the co-op leader. This way, the co-op leader can simply remove your sheet and will have an extra set of medical release forms ready to go for the parent who's replacing you. Of course, minor adjustments will have to be made for the remaining parents, but having this extra package of materials will save the co-op leader some time and energy.

We've devoted an entire chapter to creating a safe environment and handling unexpected medical emergencies (see Chapter Seventeen). We recommend that you review these safety tips at least annually with your co-op members. You could even take this task a step further by planning to attend a CPR training class together as one of your co-op outings.

Three Strikes Policy

No one likes addressing and resolving conflict. It's unpleasant and intrusive. As human beings, we naturally tend to avoid this task. However, conflict is a part of life, so it's usually best to get these problems addressed quickly so life can move on. As we've stated before, the co-op program is one that operates on respect: respect for one another's time, respect for upholding the commitments made, and respect for the rules of the program.

With this in mind, we're happy to report that in the numerous interviews conducted prior to writing this book, we only found a small handful of conflicts that have actually had to be addressed either via a general broadcast e-mail or directly with a co-op member. The most common problems that seem to surface are promptness in picking up children at the end of a shift and being present and ready to go for your designated shift.

When a co-op leader finds that a problem starts festering within the group, she needs to handle the issue as soon as it's brought to her attention. Addressing the conflict with the offending parent in a public setting is going to cause a tremendous amount of grief for all involved, so be sure to speak with this parent in a private setting. Be sensitive to the fact that the parent probably already realizes that she's stepped over the line, whether it was intentional or unintentional, and we are all human and need to be met with some degree of understanding.

The Three Strikes policy simply states that if three complaints have been shared with the leader (following the initial visit) then the parent can be asked to leave the co-op. Any remaining babysitting shifts that were on the calendar are marked as "unavailable" or picked up by another co-op member who needs to earn additional tickets. Any remaining tickets are given to the leader. Those tickets will then be redistributed to a new parent joining the group at a future time.

The Three Strikes policy should be reserved for offenses that negatively impact the group. If a co-op parent contacts the co-op leader with a relatively simple complaint (i.e. a parent is consistently running late, or one mom brought her daughter when she was sick), the co-op leader can nip the problem in the bud by putting out a friendly reminder to all the members stating, "Please remember that we all have very busy schedules and it's important to be on time." Sending out a general broadcast e-mail won't make anyone feel singled out. The offending parent will probably recognize that she needs to be more thoughtful and will hopefully realize that improving her punctuality is far easier than giving up the benefits of the co-op program.

If the problem is of greater magnitude, be prompt in addressing this problem when it first takes place. Addressing the issue may require a thoughtful visit over the phone or a one-on-one meeting to see that the issue is resolved. An infraction which might require this type of disciplinary action could be a parent forgetting that, let's say, Friday mornings are her co-op mornings. This parent may keep missing her shift because she recently joined the local gym and is making the gym a higher priority. If she forgets her shift three times, then it's in the best interest of the entire group to ask her to step out of co-op. Chances are good that she knows she's been breaking the rules, and this visit won't come as a surprise.

Is approaching this situation difficult? Absolutely. However, allowing this offending parent to remain in the group isn't the answer. There may be other parents who've been affected by her behavior and just haven't brought this fact to your attention. As a result, parents will stop using her shifts, and slowly but surely, this will become a hindrance to the program.

When the group initially comes together for the start-up meeting, address the fact that repeated offenses affect everyone and that when problems persist, a co-op member can and should be asked to leave the group. Then take a moment to introduce the Three Strikes policy and make sure that everyone is comfortable with the guidelines that are established for this aspect of the program. Remember that there aren't many problems that can't be worked out with a little tact and understanding.

If you must ask a parent to leave, state that you don't think that co-op is working very well for her at this time in her life and that her "unavailability" is causing some problems for the rest of the group.

Maybe she's overcommitted her time with schooling, volunteering services, or an increasingly difficult family situation. Or, maybe she's had personal matters that have made it difficult for her to be reliable. Whatever the case may be, try to handle the situation in a way where both parties are able to maintain their dignity, and then use discretion when updating the group on the new changes.

Keep in mind that these are just a sample of some rules that you can implement. It is important to customize your own babysitting co-op rules to meet the needs of your individual group. When establishing your own rules, be open and honest about your feelings and desires. The rules are there to provide you with peace of mind while creating a happy, comfortable and safe environment for everyone.

Establish Rules for Babysitters Summary

Establishing a clear set of rules ensures that co-op members know what's expected of them and reduces opportunities for conflict. Review the rules point by point at your meeting, staying open to changes that your co-op members want to make. Be thoughtful with your approach when rules are broken. Make sure to handle discussions about broken rules in a private setting, respecting the privacy of those involved. Review your outlined rules at each calendaring meeting and ask if anyone wants to discuss or adjust particular rules.

CHAPTER 8
EXPECTING A BABY

Babysitting co-ops and young families go hand-in-hand. In fact, the reason babysitting co-op exists is because we're in the business of creating and raising children. If you are one of those moms who might still be looking forward to expanding your family, we wish you the best. There's nothing more exhilarating than learning that you're expecting and then welcoming a beautiful new child into your family. And at the same time, there's nothing more exhausting than being pregnant and adapting to the schedule of a precious newborn.

When news comes that a co-op member is expecting a new baby, be prepared to make some adjustments. Your newly pregnant friend may find that she's terribly ill during those early months. And once she finally feels like she's got her burst of energy back, she may start feeling very tired as she enters the final trimester. Certainly, we've all been there and can lend a sympathetic ear when these days are challenging. When this time comes, and it will come, here's the best way to address this much needed time off.

Taking Time Off

First of all, the pregnant mom needs to be sensitive to her needs and know that she can take a few months off from co-op and then return when the time is right. The beauty of the co-op program is that it can be as flexible as it needs to be given the dynamics of your group. So, don't worry that your friends will think less of you if you're not fully participating until the day you deliver.

Most moms decide to temporarily step out of co-op three to four weeks prior to delivery so they can have time to rest and get things ready for the baby. This time frame varies with each mom, and the exact date should not be set in stone. Decide on a date when you think you'll be ready for some time off and then be prepared to share this date with your group at the next calendaring meeting. When your group comes together and the calendar is assembled, remind the co-op leader that you'll be opting out of co-op following your chosen date. The co-op leader can then give the other parents a chance to fill your vacant shifts if someone is looking for extra babysitting opportunities. If parents aren't able to fill in those babysitting shifts, then the co-op leader will simply mark them as unavailable from that time forward.

Prior to the baby's arrival, take some time to determine when you will want to jump back into co-op. Again, share this date with your co-op leader, and she can put you down on the calendar noting that your shift may be considered tentative during those first few weeks of your return. Communicating your tentative status can be accomplished in a couple of different ways. The co-op leader can either write the word tentative, next to your name, or simply place an asterisk next to your name noting its significance at the bottom of the calendaring page.

Using Co-op During Your Time Off

Feel free to utilize the babysitting co-op program during your time off. Certainly, you've put forth the effort to provide babysitting services and to earn much needed tickets. Having those tickets at your disposal will be important when you find that you need some extra rest in the middle of the day. With this in mind, however, we want to remind the expecting mothers to use their discretion in determining how many tickets to keep in reserve. Keeping too many tickets out of circulation can greatly affect how well the program operates. Try to be sensitive not only to your needs, but also to the needs of the group.

Holding tickets in reserve and then slowly putting them back into circulation is a perfectly fine idea. However, if you know (or suspect) that you'll be opting out of co-op for good, then you need to be prepared to return the amount of tickets which were originally given to you when you first joined the co-op program. As a courtesy, you should let your co-op leader know that you're looking to step out of co-op for good. Other parents may be waiting to join the group and you wouldn't want this delayed information to cause grief for the co-op group as a whole. If you find that you've set a return date and then realize that returning isn't a realistic option, make it a point to communicate this information in a timely manner as well.

Returning to Co-op

It will take some time for you to get back into the groove of providing care for other children during your normally scheduled shift. Adjusting to the new demands of an infant isn't easy at first. Take it slow and only accept the number of kids that you feel you can reasonably handle. Be careful not to be overzealous in your desire to operate at full capacity. No one expects you to care for the number of children you were used to watching prior to having your baby. Reducing the number of hours of your shift, or the frequency of your shift is also very understandable. Talk with you co-op leader and make the necessary adjustments as needed.

Now that your little one is here, you're entitled to additional tickets so you can enjoy the benefits of having this child become a part of the co-op program. If your baby comes in the middle of a calendaring segment, you may need to remind the co-op leader to prepare and provide you with additional tickets. Find some quiet time for yourself and use the additional tickets. Your little one will be just fine. You're actually doing yourself and your baby a favor. Truth be told, we just can't do it all. It's important to make our own needs a priority as well, and by taking some time for yourself, you'll return feeling refreshed and ready to enjoy those precious parenting moments between mother and child.

It's important to also realize that leaving your new baby may be hard in the beginning. This feeling is completely natural. Take comfort in knowing that the co-op members are your friends and they wouldn't be a part of your group if you didn't trust their abilities and their judgment. At first, most co-op parents tend to schedule co-op time for their other children and will take the new infant with them as they run errands or meet appointments. However, when you're ready, and you feel your baby is old enough, let your friends give you a hand for a couple of hours. If need be, make those first few outings short ones. With time, your little one will grow accustomed to having other parents feeding him a bottle and even napping happily at someone else's home.

Expecting a Baby Summary

Expectant co-op members should plan to take some time off prior to and following their deliveries. The amount of time off may vary from woman to woman. Vacant shifts can be filled by members who are looking for extra babysitting hours. If no one wants to fill them, write "unavailable" on those shifts on the calendar. Members who are stepping out of co-op on a temporary basis may still use the co-op's babysitting services because they have already provided babysitting services with the intent of spending their tickets once again. Mothers who decide not to return to the co-op after the arrival of their babies need to return the original amount of tickets they were given when they joined the co-op.

CHAPTER 9
STAYING CONNECTED IN THE CO-OP

As co-op members, we show up on each other's doorsteps frequently, but seldom spend much time together at the beginning or end of these shifts. Our conversations are usually limited to exchanging information about snacks and diapers. While the kids are building great relationships by playing with one another, the connections between co-op parents can sometimes be overlooked and set aside.

One of the most common concerns we hear from co-op parents is that they may not know some of the other parents as well as they'd like to before leaving their children there for a period of time. Naturally, parents gravitate toward people they already know, and this is particularly true when it comes to scheduling babysitting time. However, sticking to the few parents that you already know within your social circle can create an imbalance within the co-op and may lead to some of the parents feeling like they're always out on the fringe. Often times, what co-op parents really need is just some solid quality time to get to know each other better, increasing their level of comfort with all the co-op members.

What's the solution to this problem? Organize some social gatherings where parents can sit around and talk about their latest activities, common parenting challenges, current community events, or the upcoming playoffs. These gatherings don't need to be fancy or long, but should be comfortable enough so that everyone feels included. When you find yourselves together, make it a point to draw newer co-op members into the conversation. Ask them questions about themselves, their families, and particular interests. Focusing some of the attention on the newer members will help them feel integrated much quicker. And it will also help you to broaden your social circle.

Planning activities that are kid-friendly means that all of the parents can participate. The purpose of these events is to bring the group together and have a good time while strengthening friendships.

A great way to make sure that social events happen regularly is to invite one co-op member to take the lead in planning two to three activities for each calendaring segment. Throw out a few ideas to your group during a planning session and then be sure to set a date so that everyone can plan to attend. Acting as the events coordinator doesn't have to be a permanent assignment; however, someone needs to take the lead in order to get the ball rolling.

If you're looking for a little bit of guidance on how to get started, you won't have to look any further. We've devoted the remainder of this chapter to some creative and cost effective activities.

Kid Friendly Activities

Playgroups
Playgroups are designated meeting times when parents and children come together. The children play, and the parents talk. Playgroups work especially well for parents with preschool-aged children. During the winter months take turns hosting the playgroup in each of your homes. However, when the weather warms up, meet at a park and make it a lunch date for the kids. Try setting one particular day and time aside each month. You're more likely to start getting regular attendees when the schedule is consistent. With the children working out their extra energy on the monkey bars, parents can sit and enjoy the sunshine and each other's company.

Potlucks
Potlucks are a fun way to include older children who aren't home during normal co-op hours. Just a few potluck dinners a year can really bring a group together. Build your dinner around a theme or an event such as the 4th of July. Involving working spouses and older siblings also makes the co-op feel like a family affair, instead of just an activity that the at-home parent and the younger kids do during the day.

A Day at the Zoo

Attending the zoo is a great way to spend your time. Most community zoos are fairly inexpensive and if the cost is more than you'd like to spend, call and ask them if they offer discount days or group rates. Take advantage of letting the animals on display do the entertaining.

Nature Walk

This activity is one that can take place more than once a year and doesn't have to be extravagant. With a bag in hand, take a casual walk around your neighborhood. It doesn't take much to impress children, and with the varieties of colorful leaves and flowers in bloom, you may just find yourself impressed as well. If you have older children in your co-op, you can take this activity a step further and have them create a collection that will proudly be displayed on the outside of their bedroom door for weeks to come.

Holiday Parties

Along the same lines, holiday parties make fun traditions for co-op groups. Besides Christmas parties, you could get together on Halloween, the 4th of July, or Valentine's Day. In areas where trick-or-treating isn't practical, a Halloween party might fill an important need for your little angels and devils as well as your co-op parents.

Parent Friendly Activities

Dessert Night

There's nothing like getting out with a group of friends and digging into a rich, chocolaty sundae. Don't worry about those extra calories. How often do you really get to sit down and let someone else bring you your favorite treat? This activity seems to be a good one to schedule on weeknights during the school year. Plan to meet at a favorite restaurant after your family's had dinner and the kids are put to bed so you can enjoy some overdue adult conversation. You can feel completely guilt free about sneaking away for an hour or two because you know that everyone's needs have been met and they are safe and sound at home with your spouse or a friend.

Book Club

Book club is a great way to build stronger friendships because it automatically creates a commonality among all the members. Additionally, you're inviting people to step out of their comfort zone and explore a variety of concepts and issues that are going to help you see a completely new side of their personalities. Running a book club doesn't take much effort. Designate one night each month that will always be your book club night, and keep the meeting time consistent (for example, the second Tuesday of each month at 7:00 p.m.). Prior to holding your first book club meeting, ask everyone to come with two or three books to propose. Once everyone has had a chance to share their books, plug one title in for each month. If your book falls in January, then you would host the group at your home as well as lead a thought provoking discussion. Many library websites have book club discussion guides for well-known books. Additionally, some publishers include book club discussion guides as an appendix.

Back to School Party
There's nothing in the world like sending your children back to school at the end of a long summer break. If your kids are anything like ours, they're bursting at the seams to purchase their school supplies and get back to playing dodge ball on the playground. Plus, our kids get to return to school feeling a bit more accomplished because they're moving up a grade, which also means they're moving up in their social standing as well. But why does all the excitement and anticipation have to be focused around our children? As parents, we should observe this rite of passage as well. After school has been underway for a few weeks, invite all your friends to come together and celebrate the fact that you've survived another summer. Once again, the school year is off to a successful start, thanks to you! Plan some simple activities that revolve around some overdue pampering and delicious treats.

Craft Day Extravaganza
Do you have a closet full of unfinished projects? Is your first child's baby book waiting for finishing touches even though he's turned seven? Are you still working on homemade Christmas stockings that were going to be ready for Christmas last year? If any of this sounds somewhat familiar then a craft day extravaganza just might be in order. Here's a fun activity that requires minimal investments and yields terrific results. Find a day on your school calendar when all the kids are out and take advantage of scheduling high school babysitters for an afternoon. What's required in order to pull these events together? A few clean tabletops with lots of working space and fun music. If you're planning to host a lunch with your event, invite others to bring rolls, a pot of soup, or some finger sandwiches so you don't have to worry about all the details. Yes, this activity will require paying

the high school aged babysitter, but sometimes it's worth it!

Couples Game Night

Hosting a game night is an excellent way to help create a feeling of unity. This will not only benefit the co-op group as a whole, but may also enhance your personal relationship as well. There are a couple of ways to approach this activity. One approach might be to have the game night focused around a theme, such as South of the Border Fiesta, Mardi Gras Madness, or a Tailgating Party. Another easy way to add some pizzazz is to plan your game night around a holiday such as Valentine's Day, New Year's Eve, or April Fool's Day. While creating a theme for your party can be a lot of fun, it isn't a must. The real goal here is to create an inviting atmosphere so that everyone can get to know one another better. Regardless of the approach that you choose to take, keep things simple. All you really need for a successful party is a few fun games, some lively music, and simple refreshments.

Other Activities

With time, your co-op will feel like a very cohesive group, and you'll have a strong sense of connection. While social gatherings are important, there's also much to be gained by becoming aware of the needs within your group and then reaching out to others. Here are a few more suggestions to help you put your cooperative efforts to good use.

As a co-op, you could organize a clothing exchange. Plan a day or time when everyone comes together to swap extra children's or maternity clothes that aren't currently in use. You could set it up so that everyone gets their items back after they're used, or you might just treat all items like contributions. Such an exchange cuts down on individual families' storage requirements and can save everyone a lot of money as well.

In the same vein, set up a toy or baby equipment exchange. New toys are always more fun than old ones, but you don't necessarily need to go out and buy new toys. Just rotate them among the group and the kids won't ever get bored with what they have to play with. Likewise, let your group know if you have a baby crib or a changing table you're not using. Instead of taking your baby equipment to a thrift store when you're done with it, trade it for something you need. In a group of families all raising children, you're sure to find what you're looking for.

When a member of your group has a baby, take turns dropping off warm dinners for her for a week or two. Offer some ticket-free babysitting for her other children or get together and throw a baby shower.

When your group has become adept at caring for each other, turn outwards and see how you can make a difference. Take the kids Christmas caroling at a nursing home, and watch their confidence grow as they see how much their small efforts are appreciated. As a group, deliver goodies to a new family. Adopt a needy family for Secret Santa and all chip in to provide gifts. Let this newfound sense of community reach beyond the boundaries of co-op to touch the lives of those around you.

Staying Connected Summary

Plan regularly scheduled activities to help co-op members feel integrated. Plan some activities that include the whole family and some activities just for adults. These activities don't have to require much cost, but they yield long lasting results for all. Consider planning a service project so your co-op can give back to the community.

CHAPTER 10
WEEKEND CO-OP

With the weekend in sight, you breathe a sigh of relief. The week has been a busy one; most of them are. You've diligently helped the kids with their homework, taken them to ballet class, and even managed to get the oil changed. So now it's your turn to have some peace and quiet and reacquaint yourself with that other adult that roams the house. Or if you're the only adult in the house, it's time to get out and visit with some good friends. Coming up with a way to enjoy your weekend usually isn't the hardest part of the equation. Rather, finding an available babysitter will determine whether your evening out ends up being an evening in.

Let's set the scene for a typical date night in the Terry household. Ben and Rachel Terry haven't been on a date in about five months for a couple of reasons: it's cost prohibitive and they just never seem to get around to planning it until it's too late.

But tonight they've managed to pull it together. Rachel called a neighborhood teenager Friday after school to ask if she could baby-sit on such short notice. If the conversation below sounds a bit familiar, it's probably because we've all had this exchange at some point and time in our parenting years.

"Hi, Katie, this is Rachel Terry. I was wondering if you could baby-sit tonight from six to ten o'clock."

"Um, I think so," Katie says.

"Do you need to check?" Rachel asks.

"I'll be right back," Katie says, and then Rachel hears shouting and something about her bedroom being cleaned.

"Yeah, I can do it," Katie says to Rachel.

"Great. So I'll pick you up a little before six, okay?"

As an afterthought, Rachel asks, "By the way, what do you charge for three children?"

To which Katie casually responds, "Eight dollars an hour."

Rachel almost chokes on her chewing gum but feels that her hands are tied. She was excited to get away with her husband, so she accepts the fact that this evening will be a spendy one. Plus, chances of her finding another sitter at this late time are slim to none.

After Rachel hangs up the phone, she takes a moment to see how much tonight is going to cost. Childcare will come to: $32. They wanted to go to dinner and a movie. Dinner would probably be $40 and the movie would be at least $20. When all is said and done, she realizes she'll be paying over $90 for one night out. No wonder they rarely go out; they can't afford it.

Rachel rushes around to make a quick dinner for the kids and cleans up the house so Katie will have a good standard of what Rachel expects when she returns. She copies down a few phone numbers, neighbors' names in case she can't be reached, and then moves on to the next task at hand. She lays out the kids' pajamas and puts all of the diapering supplies in an easy-to-find location. She finishes by making a schedule that includes dinner, cleanup, and the bedtime routine.

When Katie arrives, the kids are excited to see her and everything seems to be under control. Rachel breathes a sigh of relief and hopes for the best with her fourteen-year-old sitter. Rachel then realizes how long it's been since she's eaten an entire meal without interruptions. It will be so nice to be out, just the two of them. The only things requiring her attention are her charming husband and her shrimp scampi.

Now that she is away, she just can't seem to get rid of those nagging worries. What if Katie doesn't keep the front door locked and Spencer wanders out the front door? What if one of the kids falls down the stairs and breaks an arm? Would Katie know what to do? What if Katie ignores the kids all night and they destroy the house?

While Ben takes care of the check at the restaurant, Rachel slips away and calls home. With no answer, she becomes worried and calls again.

"Oh hi, Mrs. Terry,"

"Hi Katie. Is everything going okay?"

"Yep."

"Any problems?"

"Nope," replies Katie.

"Is everyone happy?" Rachel asks.

"I think so," Katie says. Rachel, hoping to hear more than a two to three word response, wraps up her call and tries to enjoy the rest of her night.

When Rachel and Ben return home the first thing they encounter is a kitchen table full of dirty dishes and leftover food that has been sitting out for at least three hours. The kitchen floor has crumbs and toys all over it, and there are candy wrappers on the counter next to about ten dirty cups. The baby is asleep in bed, but the other two are still awake. They're in their room, for which Rachel is grateful, but they're playing, and their teeth have not been brushed.

They find Katie in front of the T.V., toys scattered around her on the sofa and floor.

"How did it go?" Rachel asks her.

"Oh, fine,"

Rachel angrily writes her a check for $32 and then takes her home while Ben puts the older two kids to bed.

Rachel spends the next hour cleaning the kitchen and the rest of the house. "What in the world did we pay her for?" she wonders. "There has got to be a better answer than this." And there is.

We must admit that we've had some great experiences with teenage babysitters on the weekends, but unfortunately those experiences are hit and miss. Additionally, is it ever truly possible to feel completely comfortable leaving our children with teenagers? One night, when Rachel told her five-year-old who the babysitter would be, he responded, "But she's just a kid." That statement didn't instill much confidence, to say the least.

Our answer to this quandary is to organize a weekend babysitting co-op. Extending your current babysitting co-op to include Friday and Saturday nights is easy and will save you a lot of money and frustration. Having read this far in the book, you're already well aware of the benefits such a co-op provides. To help you see it in your mind, and to give Rachel and Ben a happy ending, here's the scene you would encounter at their house several months later, after Rachel and three of her friends have organized a weekend co-op.

"Do you guys remember what tonight is?" Rachel asks her children.

"It's date night!" The children jump up and down.

"Where is it tonight?" one of them asks.

"At the Meyer's house," Rachel tells them.

"All right! Josh said we get to have popcorn and watch *Toy Story*."

"Great," says Rachel. "Let's get ready and go."

The kids change into their pajamas while Rachel changes the baby and packs the diaper bag. As soon as Ben gets home they all climb into the car and drive to the Meyer's house where they see another car arriving too.

"There's Mikey," one of the kids shouts and points to another pajama-clad child walking up to the front door. The kids get out of the car and run up to the front door.

Miriam and Kent Meyers are the parents who are watching all the kids tonight. Rachel quickly exchange a few details about where she and Ben are going and ensures that Miriam has her phone number handy, which is listed on the Contact List, just in case they're needed. The kids immediately settle in with their Friday night friends, talking about their week's activities and get excited to eat dinner all together.

Rachel and Ben leave feeling calm and content. Rachel doesn't worry like she used to. She has the peace of mind knowing her children are in the care of trusted friends who have children of their own.

When they return, the kids are all lying on the floor in the family room, all in their pajamas curled up on pillows and blankets. They've watched *Toy Story*, and now Miriam is reading a story to the few who are still awake.

Rachel and Ben thank their friends and then carry their tired and happy children to the car. When they get home to their still-clean house, they lay the children down in their beds and enjoy the moment. The night has been a success. They now have three date-nights a month available without having to write any checks. And the best part is, their children look forward to Friday nights as their own special time with their friends.

Co-op parents already recognize the value that a daytime co-op provides. Now with a date night co-op in place, their full-time working spouse also gets to experience these benefits as well. Here are some quotes from a few co-op dads who really appreciate it:

- "I like that co-op is free."
- "I like that there are responsible adults watching the children instead of a teenager. The adults know what the children need."
- "No longer do I have to spend my time shuttling a babysitter back and forth."
- "I like that we come home to a house that isn't wrecked."
- "You have the option of staying home for your date if you want to."
- "We can take care of home improvement projects if we want to without having to stop and find snacks for the kids or remind them to not touch the wet paint."

In this section of the book, we have provided two different models for a weekend co-op. The first model, The Weekend Ticket Method, is an offshoot from the babysitting co-op explained earlier in the book. It can be used independent of a daytime co-op program or as an extension of an existing babysitting co-op.

Weekend co-op tickets have been created and can be found in Chapter Fourteen. While these tickets are different than the daytime co-op tickets the exchange system remains the same. Printing these tickets on a different colored card stock is a good way to keep the two sets of tickets separate. Just as with the daytime program, the babysitting co-op parent opens up her home and watches those children along with her own at her home.

The second model, The Date Night Rotation Method, is run differently, with tickets not being required. The calendar is your only means of keeping track of the schedule. The babysitting hours can either operate on a set timetable or be flexible and compliment the needs of the parents who are going out for the night. How you want your schedule to unfold is something that should be discussed upfront and with all the participating adults present. Here again, the parents who are going out for the evening will bring their children to your home to be cared for in your environment.

When it comes to implementing any of the above programs it is important that there is a high level of trust and familiarity among the adults and children since both parents will be present in those evening hours. Clearly, the weekend program requires both adults to be comfortable with the arrangements and supportive of the program. If one parent is not on board with the Weekend Co-op, you'll find that either the majority of the work falls to one person or that the other spouse may be participating, but doing so begrudgingly, which is not a desirable situation either.

Just as with the daytime co-op program, everyone should come together for a planning meeting. Establishing a clear understanding of the rules and expectations for the Weekend Co-op Program is essential in guaranteeing a happy experience for all. When you meet, you will want to ensure that all of the families share the same parenting and disciplining philosophies. Determine how you are going to handle potential conflicts in advance so it will not be uncomfortable when situations present themselves. Additionally, be sure to sit with your children before taking them to their friends home and let them know that all the adults understand how things will play out for the evening. Establishing this groundwork ahead of time will help your children to also have a successful experience while they are out of your care.

Now let's discuss the details of these two models so that you and your friends can determine which system best accommodates your needs. Regardless of the method you choose to follow, we're sure you'll find that the time with your spouse, will work wonders for your sanity, family life and wallet as well.

Weekend Co-op Option 1 – The Weekend Ticket Method

The Weekend Ticket Method is an extension of the original babysitting co-op concept discussed earlier in this book. Nothing changes with the rules and principles of this co-op except for the fact that you'll be exchanging what we call "Weekend Tickets" instead of regular co-op tickets as noted above. Your weekend co-op consists of only those members who want to take the regular co-op a step further for their weekend events. This group of parents will become a "new co-op," if you will, unto themselves.

The advantage that comes with the weekend co-op is that it's meant to offer parents some flexible hours that can be used for a variety of activities. The Weekend Co-Op can save families a tremendous amount of money. And, it can be used for more than just a quiet dinner away from home. We've talked with a number of parents who like to use the weekend co-op to finish up home improvement projects such as staining a fence, painting, or laying tile in their kitchen. Any parent can appreciate how tricky completing these types of projects can be when your children want to be an active part of the home improvement team. Other co-op parents have found that weekend co-op can be a real life saver when they're finishing up a term paper or trying to take advantage of working some overtime hours.

With this in mind, it's important to remember that the weekend co-op is not necessarily something that will appeal to all the members of your group. Co-op members can only utilize the weekend co-op if they're providing weekend babysitting hours as well. As you can imagine, paying a co-op friend with weekend tickets instead of cash saves you a significant amount of babysitting money that can be spent in a number of fun ways.

Outlined below are the extra steps required to get the weekend co-op up and running. These activities only take about an additional five minutes and should be accomplished at the end of the initial planning meeting.

1.   *Identify Weekend Co-op Members* – Once you've taken care of all your daytime co-op business, the co-op leader asks who is interested in participating in the weekend co-op. These parents then break off and now become a new co-op group which operates independent of the daytime co-op. The co-op leader will add an asterisk next to your name when she puts the Contact List together to identify all the weekend participants.

Just as with the regular co-op, weekend co-op is scheduled on a first-come-first-serve basis. The same rules apply for scheduling, meals, punctuality, etc. Also, be mindful of how many kids you are comfortable accepting. Sometimes little ones can become tired and agitated as the night progresses. Having too many kids scheduled during your shift could make it difficult to comfort those who are feeling out of their element.

2.   *Calendaring* – Determine whether you want to set Friday nights or Saturdays as part of your weekend co-op calendar. Keeping this day consistent is helpful for the purpose of scheduling events or activities in the months to come. You will project your weekend babysitting shifts out for the entire calendaring period just as you did with the daytime program. Be sure to take a look at any upcoming holidays or school breaks to see if you need to block out any particular dates. If you need a quick review on how to incorporate a weekend co-op calendar, take a look at the sample calendars that are provided on pages 34 and 36.

3.   *Babysitting Order* – With your weekend parents in place, start at the beginning of the calendar and place each parent's name in the Friday or Saturday slot. This is now considered your weekend shift. Be sure to rotate the names in an orderly fashion so that one parent doesn't end up with too many shifts too close together.

4.   *Determine Hours* – It's usually best to approach weekend co-op hours with some flexibility because of differing events. However, if you are a fan of adhering to a strict schedule, then this is the time to determine what your weekend co-op hours will be. A good four to five hour block usually allows parents enough time to take in dinner and a movie, complete a home improvement project or enjoy some quiet shopping time.

5. *Scheduling Weekend Hours* – As weekend co-op participants, it's important to establish a reasonable deadline wherein parents can contact you and schedule their night out. For example, you might decide that anyone needing to schedule weekend co-op time must call by Friday morning, 9:00 a.m. The group should agree upon a specific time that feels fair for all involved. The weekend babysitter is then committed to being available for her shift until that appointed time. If that time comes and goes and no one has contacted the weekend babysitter, the weekend babysitter is free to make weekend plans of her own. Remember to check your messages frequently and return calls as your shift draws closer. Parents will be anxious to take advantage of some quiet adult time out.

6. *Payment* – On the following page, you'll find an additional template for the weekend tickets. The ticket distribution and exchange operates in the same fashion as it does with the daytime co-op. The same rules apply with these tickets (i.e. payment for meals or tardiness). The only difference is that these tickets are only good among the weekend co-op members and for weekend babysitting time. We recommend producing these weekend tickets on a different color of cardstock so that they're easy to identify and won't become mixed up with your daytime co-op tickets.

7. *Rules* – The rules for the weekend co-op shouldn't vary too far from the rules that are in place for daytime co-op. However, if you feel more comfortable adding a few new rules (that address evening concerns) this is certainly an option. Some additional rules that are a bit more "weekend specific" can be found at the end of the following section.

Weekend Co-op	Weekend Co-op
1 Hour Ticket	**1 Hour Ticket**
Weekend Co-op	Weekend Co-op
Weekend Co-op	Weekend Co-op
1 Hour Ticket	**1 Hour Ticket**
Weekend Co-op	Weekend Co-op
Weekend Co-op	Weekend Co-op
1 Hour Ticket	**1 Hour Ticket**
Weekend Co-op	Weekend Co-op
Weekend Co-op	Weekend Co-op
1/2 Hour Ticket	**1/2 Hour Ticket**
Weekend Co-op	Weekend Co-op
Weekend Co-op	Weekend Co-op
1/2 Hour Ticket	**1/2 Hour Ticket**
Weekend Co-op	Weekend Co-op

Weekend Co-op Option 2 – The Date Night Rotation Method

The Date Night Rotation Method resembles the Weekend Ticket Method in several ways: no money is exchanged for childcare services and members meet ahead of time to set up the calendar and discuss other details. However, with the Date Night Rotation Method, no tickets are exchanged, and each couple has pre-designated nights for babysitting and leaving their children with other co-op members. Additionally, many children may be present at the same time, so you'll need the support and assistance of your spouse or another adult.

If you're looking for a good "stand-alone" co-op program that is only needed for the weekend hours, then this is a good one to consider. This is a great option for families with two working adults who are not available to work babysitting shifts during the day. The advantages of the Date Night Rotation Method are that it allows you to get out more often and seems to work well for smaller groups. With this method in place, you can have three nights out per month with only having to babysit once within that same month. However, if you want to keep your weekends open or flexible, the Weekend Ticket Method may be the better option.

Let's start at the beginning.

Who Should Be Part of Your Weekend Co-op?

When thinking about whom you should invite to participate in your Date Night Co-op, think long and hard about the mix of children. With the Weekend Ticket Method, only a few of the co-op children will be together at any given time. The Date Night Rotation Method, however, allows for three additional couples to bring their children to you during your particular shift. This means that there could be several children together for several hours every weekend. It is important that you have a nice blend of ages and personalities since this will now be a part of their weekend routine.

Therefore, keep these factors in mind:
* *Age Compatibility.* Children in approximately the same age group will enjoy each other's company more than children spread out over many years. A lone fifth grader will not be happy with a group of toddlers.
* *Effort Required.* One group we know of operated extremely well

until three of the four couples had babies within several months of each other. This group found that it was impossible for two adults to care for several newborns as well as a group of preschoolers.

- *Personalities.* Most children will get along well with others their age. But if you know of an irreconcilable personality conflict between two children, it's better to steer clear of the situation and pre-empt disaster.
- *Reliability and Trustworthiness of Parents.* They're your friends, so you know their habits. If one of your friends is consistently late or takes advantage of others, she may not be the best candidate for your co-op.

How Many Members?

How many members you invite depends upon the type of schedule you'd like to keep. Some co-ops have only two families involved, and each couple has one to two date nights per month. This is a low-impact way to go, but you may need and want more nights out than this.

For the sake of simplicity in our example, we'll use a co-op group of four families. This way, each couple gets three date nights a month and spends one night watching everyone else's children. For months which include a fifth weekend, you could just take the last weekend off.

Initial Planning Meeting

When you invite your friends to the initial planning meeting, ask them to bring their calendars/planners or whatever they use to keep track of their family activities. At the initial planning meeting, your co-op will make several decisions. Here is a sample agenda. A reproducible agenda is included at the end of this chapter.

1. Introductions: It's likely that everyone will know each other, but if you have invited a new person to join from the neighborhood, make introductions all around.
2. Calendar
3. Rules/Guidelines
4. Medical Forms & Contact Lists

After this initial meeting, the leader (you, if you're starting this co-op) will type up the agreed-upon rules and guidelines and make copies for everyone, along with a copy of each family's medical form for every household. Putting these items in a clearly marked folder will make organization easier for everyone.

Let's go over each item on the agenda more in depth, minus the introductions.

Calendar

Contact the friends that you've invited to join the co-op and let them know when and where you'll be holding your first meeting. Remind your friends to bring their calendars along as well. This will help things to run smoother when planning your co-op calendar. See Chapter Five for a review of calendaring options. If you need to bring your children along in order to get things up and running, have a really fun movie with snacks ready to go!

Your goal for this part of the meeting is to come up with a schedule that looks like this:

1st Friday: Thompsons
2nd Friday: Landrys
3rd Friday: Nielsens
4th Friday: Terrys

It looks simple enough, but getting there requires a couple of steps. First of all, decide on a night of the week for date night. Fridays or Saturdays are the days of choice for most groups, but you'll need to decide on one and stick to it. If you try to go back and forth, or make your schedule varied, such as 1st Saturday, 2nd Friday, 3rd Friday, 4th Saturday, everyone will be perpetually confused. Just pick one and stick with it.

After you've chosen a day of the week, each couple needs to be committed to watching all the other kids on one of those nights. In our example, the Thompsons will be the babysitters the first week, the Landrys the second week, and so on.

You'll also need to come up with hours of operation. At first, it may be difficult to gauge just how long is long enough, and, conversely, how long is too long. So you may want to tentatively set hours in the beginning and then regroup after a month to decide if your hours need to be adjusted.

To begin with, we suggest a 6 to 9 o'clock shift. This may not be quite enough time for dinner and a movie, but if all goes well at the babysitters' house, you can soon work up either starting earlier or pushing your ending time out even later if everyone agrees.

There will be times when scheduling conflicts come up. We'll talk about resolutions to those conflicts in the Rules Section.

Rules & Guidelines

Because it can be hard to think up rules for a program you haven't yet tried, we've included a checklist of possible rules. All you have to do is go down the checklist in your meeting and mark the ones that apply to your group.
- Always feed children before you drop them off.
- Always plan on the kids eating at the babysitters' house.
- Drop off no later than 6:15 p.m., so dinner can get underway for the children.
- Arrive to pick up kids again at or before the ending time.
- Call if you're going to be late.
- Make sure both babysitters are at the house at all times.
- Don't leave the babysitters' house without leaving a phone number where you can be reached for the evening.
- Have children wear their pajamas to the babysitters' house.
- Leave any special toys, books or other treasures at home.
- One movie is allowed per evening.
- No movies, television, gaming devices or use of computers allowed.
- Try to get the children to sleep when you're the babysitter.
- Children may go outside to play.
- Children may only watch preapproved films.
- Timeouts are permissible for discipline.
- Babysitters are responsible to any damage to their homes that occurs on their watch.

Medical Forms & Contact Lists

Each couple should have a copy of a medical form for the children in your co-op. This medical form will be essential if the child is sick or injured and must be taken to the emergency room while the parents are away. Additionally, make sure you have a current Contact List attached to your Medical Release forms so you can reach an alternate relative or friend if needed.

It's simplest to have all the parents fill out the Medical Release forms and the Contact List at the initial meeting. Someone can then take all the forms and make enough copies for each couple to have on hand as a precautionary measure.

We've included a Medical Release form and a Contact List on pages 103-104 that you can photocopy and provide for parents to complete at the initial meeting.

Getting Started

After your group has everything organized and everyone is aware of the calendar assignments and their responsibilities, it's time to start the fun. We suggest starting at the beginning of a month so everyone starts off on the same foot. Introduce your children to the concept by explaining to them it's a special party for them, a party that's sort of like a sleepover, only they won't spend the whole night there.

Chapter Eighteen is a great resource for you to use when hosting the children. You'll find kid-friendly dinner menus, appropriate movies for different age groups, and tips for helping kids feel comfortable at your home when they're sleepy and their parents are still hours from returning.

We won't kid you: your babysitting nights will be tiring. But keep in mind that you'll create some great memories for your family and friends, your kids will love it, and you'll get three nights of free childcare as a bonus.

Weekend Co-op Summary

Establishing a weekend co-op is a great way to save a tremendous amount of money while finding time to get away for some adult interaction. It is easy to pull together and incorporates many of the same rules as your daytime co-op. Plus, you have the comfort of knowing that your children are being watched by responsible adults so you can fully relax and enjoy your evening out. There are two weekend co-op methods to choose from: the Weekend Ticket Method and the Date Night Rotation Method. Consider which method best suits your group, and plan accordingly. Check out Chapter Eighteen for ideas on how to host a great date night shift.

CHAPTER 11
HOW TO PERFORM THE START-UP MEETING

Congratulations on arriving to this point in the book! Together, we've covered all the important points of the program and now it's time to take the co-op concept and transform it into a viable and integral part of your life.

Everything that you need to know has been discussed in the previous chapters. And in just a few moments, you'll find a comprehensive agenda that will take you through the step-by-step process of planning and executing your start-up meeting and activities. If you've decided to invite a friend to act as a co-leader with you, now is the time to sit down together and put some names and dates on paper. Contacting your additional friends who may be interested in joining co-op is your next step. Let them know when and where you'll be holding your orientation and start-up meeting. You'll need to remind your friends to bring their personal calendars for planning purposes. See pages 28-38 for specifics on how to create a co-op calendar. Other pieces of information that will need to be brought to the meeting are the Contact List information, Medical Release information and shift preferences. Encouraging your friends to come prepared will save you quite a bit of time when you're assembling the start-up materials.

Consider holding your meeting at a time when someone else (like your spouse or a friend) can take charge of your children. The meeting will be far more effective if you can make alternate arrangements for your children while you entertain new concepts and questions. If this is not an option, don't let this stop you from getting started. Simply find a space that can be designated as a "play area," so the children will be entertained while you take care of business.

The start-up agenda on the following page takes all of the guesswork out of this initial process. We've included another copy of this agenda on page 99 for copying purposes as well. We recommend reading through the entire agenda before holding your meeting. There are a few optional activities that you may want to accomplish ahead of time. Having these tasks out of the way will help your meeting run smoother (i.e. printing out enough copies of the sample calendar for everyone to review).

Don't feel intimidated by all the points found on the start-up agenda. As we've stated before, this comprehensive agenda is here to ensure that you cover all of the points you feel might apply to your group. Once you've gone through this initial process of establishing your co-op, the co-op program tends to manage itself. With this in mind, let's get started.

Babysitting Co-op Start-up Agenda

Co-op Leader:_____

Date:_____

Remind members to bring their Contact List information, Medical Release information and personal schedules with them prior to the meeting. Make it a point to invite the co-op members to voice any questions or concerns at the end of each point on the agenda.

Understand the Co-op Concepts
Take a moment to review the following key concepts.

- *Babysitting Co-ops*
  - ➢ What is a co-op and how does it work? (Defined on page 3)
  - ➢ What are the benefits of babysitting co-ops? (See page 4)

- *Principles of Successful Babysitting Co-ops*
  - ➢ Briefly touch on the Principles of Success (See pages 39-44)

- *Role of the Co-op Leader*
  - ➢ Touch on the role/responsibilities of the Co-op Leader (See pages 14-18)

Pulling it All Together
Now that everyone understands the general concepts, let's pull your program together.

Ticket Exchange
  - ➢ Review the concept of the co-op tickets (See page 19).
  - ➢ Pass the book around and show the co-op members what the tickets will look like once they're produced (See page 106).
  - ➢ Identify the number of tickets each participant needs and jot this information down on the following page. Review *Start-up Tickets* examples if needed (See page 20).
  - ➢ Turn to page 21 and review the *Payment of Tickets* examples which show how tickets are to be exchanged.
  - ➢ Take a moment to role play a few ticket exchange.
  - ➢ Discuss the concepts of *Rounding up Your Payment, Replacing Lost Tickets, Returning Co-op Tickets* and the importance of *Keep Those Tickets Moving* (See pages 23-26).

Name & Quantity of Tickets	Name & Quantity of Tickets

- *Calendaring*
  - ➢ Make a copy of the Small Group and Large Group sample calendars found on pages 34 and 36 for each co-op member prior to your meeting.
  - ➢ Discuss what a babysitting shift is and explain how shifts will repeat themselves throughout the calendar (See pages 28-30).
  - ➢ Pass out the two sample calendars and take a moment to identify whether you'll be functioning as a Small or Large co-op group. This sample calendar also effectively shows how shifts coordinate, overlap and repeat during the course of a month.
  - ➢ Ask each parent to choose a shift and then note these shifts on a white board or poster board.
  - ➢ Be sure to note holidays, school breaks, or special events as you're discussing your upcoming calendar.
  - ➢ Invite the co-op members to break into groups based on the day of their shift. They now can fill in their shifts on the provided blank calendars.
  - ➢ Discuss the following
    - How to schedule babysitting
    - *The 30-Minute Rule*
    - Switching shifts and the importance of timely notification
    - Canceling a shift only as a last resort
  - ➢ Schedule a time six to eight weeks out to assess the program. Set a second date toward the end of your calendaring period for planning your next calendaring segment. Note this on the master co-op calendar.

- *Establishing Rules*
  - ➢ Discuss why establishing rules is a necessary part of co-op.
  - ➢ Go through the rules, emphasizing the points that are most important for your group (starting on page 47). Have someone follow along in the book noting any rule alterations on a separate sheet of paper.

➤ Discuss the importance of creating a safe environment. Review the points that are applicable from Chapter Seventeen, Babyproofing, First Aid & Safety Tips (starting on page 129).

- *Expectant Mothers*
  ➤ If applicable, discuss points in Chapter Eight (See page 57).
  ➤ These same principles can apply toward co-op members who may need to take time off due to unexpected family circumstances.

- *Staying Connected*
  ➤ Invite someone to coordinate a few social events.
  ➤ Choose one or two activities that appeal to your group and schedule them on the calendar while at this meeting.
  ➤ Review the suggested activities in Chapter Nine, Staying Connected in the Co-op (starting on page 61).

- *Weekend Co-op*
  Explain the differences between the Weekend Ticket Method (See details starting on page 73) and the Date Night Rotation Method (See details starting on page 77).
  ➤ Decide whether you'll be using a weekend co-op and then choose the method that works best as outlined in Chapter Ten.
  ➤ If you've chosen to use the Weekend Ticket Method, explain that a new set of tickets will be created and rotated only amongst the weekend co-op members. This method is an extension of the daytime co-op program and can only be used by those who are also willing to provide babysitting during the weekend hours.
  ➤ Note the weekend participants and the number of tickets needed in the space on the following page.
  ➤ If you've chosen to use the Date Night Rotation Method, explain that tickets are not necessary and that the group will operate per a set schedule. The calendar will be the main tool used for tracking this weekend schedule.
  ➤ Both programs fill the same need and can be used independent of the daytime co-op program.
  ➤ Fill in the weekend shifts on the master calendar as they apply to either the Weekend Ticket Method or the Date Night Rotation Method.

Name & Quantity of Tickets	**Name & Quantity of Tickets**

- *Part Two - Resources*
  - ➤ Invite the co-op members to ask any questions which may not have already been addressed.
  - ➤ Note the additional material found in the *Part Two - Resources* portion of this book if desired.
  - ➤ Feel free to touch quickly upon the title headings for the benefit of the entire group saving some time to explore these additional topics.
    - *Frequently Asked Questions* (See page 93)
    - *Online Resources, Apps & Forms* (Starting on page 97)
    - *Activities Kids Love* (See page 108)
    - *Healthy Snacks* (See page 121)
    - *Babyproofing, First Aid & Safety Tips* (See page 129)
    - *Ideas for Evening Activities, Dinners & Movies* (See page 141)

CHAPTER 12
WRAPPING IT UP

So there you have it. We've given you all our wisdom regarding babysitting co-ops. We hope this program becomes a cherished part of your lives as it has been in ours. In a relatively short period of time, you'll have a strong network of friends who understand and share the same co-op vision you do. You'll have a new sense of freedom that comes from rediscovering time for yourself, making better use of your finances, and having the peace of mind knowing your children are in a safe and trusted environment.

Make the most of the materials that we've included in this book. The chapter summaries ensure that you understand the main concepts, while the templates cover all those administrative aspects of your co-op program. We've provided you with these tools so that organizing yourself and your friends into a happily functioning co-op will be a cinch. Once your co-op is up and running, maintaining it won't require much time or effort at all.

Soon you and your friends will be able to echo the sentiments of Lana Hope, a long time co-op member and mother of five:

"My son is two and has Down Syndrome. While he is doing great, he has had some health conditions that make leaving him hard to do. Since I have joined the babysitting co-op, I feel confident about leaving him with other mothers rather than leaving my special needs child with a young adolescent. I have peace of mind knowing that his needs are met along with his older brother. Not only are these women co-op moms

themselves, they are my friends and love my kids. I am able to relax and not worry about his care when I am away."

Like Lana, we all have different needs when it comes to taking care of our families. So don't forget to customize your co-op to meet the needs of all the members. It's now your turn to create your own co-op, one that is unique and fosters feelings of belonging and connection.

It's a wonderful time when your children are small and at home. Our wish is that the babysitting co-op will enhance the magic of these precious years, giving you the time you need to refresh yourself, returning to your children renewed and patient, ready to enjoy each moment with them.

We wish you the very best and believe in your ability to succeed. Let us know how your co-op progresses. Feel free to send us your questions and insights as you adapt the program to fit your individual needs. We'd love to hear from you.

Warmly,

Samantha Fogg Nielsen
Rachel Tolman Terry

Baby-sittingco-op.blogspot.com
Facebook: Babysitting Co-op 101
Twitter @babysitcoop101

PART II

RESOURCES

CHAPTER 13
FREQUENTLY ASKED QUESTIONS

Is a co-op easy to run and will it really create the free time that I'm looking for?
Yes! *Babysitting Co-Op 101* solves the childcare dilemma which so many parents are facing today. This program has been implemented by hundreds of parents from all over the country and it is always met with enthusiastic praise. Take it first hand from a busy parent of four and co-owner of a successful salon business as well.

> *"I've been participating with my neighborhood babysitting co-op for years and love the freedom it affords me! The program is easy to set-up, self-maintaining and fun for everyone involved. Plus, I am able to save a significant amount of money in childcare expenses while my children get to play with their friends. The benefits of this program far outweigh the small investment which is required on my part. I have confidently recommended this program to a number of other parents who are looking for a win-win childcare solution."*

> ***Annie McGee***
> ***Lauren Grace & Co.***

The positive impact of the babysitting co-op program is also being recognized by various media sources as well. Over the years, we have had the pleasure of speaking to a number of parenting organizations, magazines and have conducted several news interviews with the NBC, CBS, ABC and FOX local news affiliates. We invite you to visit our blog at baby-sittingco-op.blogspot.com to view these interviews, parent testimonials and gain other valuable tips for your babysitting co-op.

The program works! You really can have a day to yourself, find those extra hours to wrap up unfinished projects and go to the grocery store in record speed. In fact, we (the authors) wrote the majority of *Babysitting Co-Op 101*, while our children spent time playing with friends in our very own babysitting co-op programs!

How do I handle my babysitting shift if I am expecting a baby?
Babysitting co-ops and expanding families go hand-in-hand. In fact, the reason babysitting co-op exists is because we're in the business of creating and raising children. We've devoted an entire chapter to the logistics of how to take time off and return to co-op for expectant mothers. Please take a moment to review these details in Chapter Eight, found on page 57.

If I adopt a child, gain custody, or have a new infant do I get additional tickets?
Yes. Once a new child has joined the family, you are entitled to an additional set of tickets. The number of tickets you'll receive for this new child will be the same number of tickets agreed upon when the babysitting co-op was initially started. As we noted earlier in the book, we've found eight tickets per child to be just right. Make it a point to get in touch with your co-op leader so she can get those tickets to you in a timely manner.

How should I handle my tickets if my child needs to rotate out of the babysitting co-op program or my family moves?
Because of the ever changing nature of our communities, having families come and go from co-op will be a common experience. In short, the co-op tickets were a gift of free time when the program was initially started. Regardless of whether you're moving or if your child no longer needs co-op services, you'll be responsible for returning the original amount of tickets that were allotted to you when you joined the program. Those returned tickets will then be redistributed to a new parent who may join the program at a future time. Please see Returning Your Co-op Tickets which is found in Chapter Four on page 24.

What if my tickets get lost or ruined?
If your tickets get misplaced or ruined, simply contact the babysitting co-op leader and inform her that you need a new set of tickets. This set of new tickets will be reproduced at your expense. You are allowed to

have one complimentary replacement set equaling the amount you believe you lost. After that, you are responsible for earning extra tickets on your own. For more details please review Replacing Lost Co-op Tickets which is found in Chapter Four on pages 23-24.

What if a parent calls for babysitting and my shift is already full?
If you've already reached full capacity for your babysitting shift, simply explain that unfortunately, your shift is already booked for the day. Then suggest that the parent try contacting another member of the babysitting co-op. Chances are good someone else may be interested in earning extra tickets outside of their scheduled shift. After a few weeks of operation, co-op members will come to know which parents are able and willing to take on extra babysitting shifts and which parents prefer not to do so.

What if a parent fails to honor her shift or the agreed upon rules for co-op?
If it becomes apparent that a particular co-op member is no longer committed to supporting your co-op program, these concerns should be immediately shared with the co-op leader. A parent who fails to meet her babysitting shift, or is chronically breaking the rules, is going to have a devastating impact on the effectiveness of the program and needs to be invited to withdraw in a timely manner.

While it may be difficult for the co-op leader to approach a friend with these concerns, it is imperative that the matter be resolved quickly. If the situation is not addressed, other co-op members may grow resentful of these infractions and it could negatively impact the integrity of the program. That said, we are happy to report that this type of behavior doesn't seem to happen on a frequent basis. In fact, we only came across one co-op leader who's ever had to address this type of behavior in her seven year co-op history.

What if a child is injured while being babysat?
If a child has an accident while in your care, you should immediately contact the parent or the emergency contact name found on your Contact List. If the accident requires immediate medical assistance, always seek medical care first and then contact the parent as soon as possible. For more specific information on how to handle first aid issues, please see Chapter Seventeen, found on page 129.

What role does homeowner's insurance play if a child is injured while at my home?

Homeowner's insurance policies are designed to protect your dwelling, personal property and family from financial disasters. Most homeowner's insurance policies include a minimum of $100,000 liability coverage for accidents or injuries that may occur to others while at your home. Liability coverage is specifically designed to cover medical expenses for individuals outside your immediate family. For your protection and peace of mind, it is highly recommended that you review your current policy to confirm the details about your liability coverage. Ensuring that your policy contains liability coverage will provide you with peace of mind and a safety net should an accident ever occur.

CHAPTER 14
ONLINE RESOURCES, APPS & FORMS

If you're like us, you turn to the Internet for ideas, tips, recipes, and advice from the experts. With blogs and social media, it's easy to find others who share your interests and have answers to the questions that plague you. For this reason, we've created internet resources to help you as you establish your babysitting co-op.

Blog
http://baby-sittingco-op.blogspot.com

We've stocked our blog with tips and helps on the following topics.
• Discipline strategies
• Activities
• Snacks
• Babysitting co-op basics
We encourage you to join in on the discussions on the blog. Share your own insights, and find out what other co-op parents have learned. But don't stop there. The *Babysitting Co-op 101* community extends to social media. We hope to see you there, too.

Facebook
Find us on Facebook: BabysittingCo-op101

We hope you'll join our community on Facebook so we can hear from you and learn about your co-op. Share pictures and videos of your co-op, join in the discussions, and let us know how you're doing.

Twitter
@BabysittingCo-op101

Follow us on Twitter for updates on co-op news, tasty snack recipes, activity ideas, and media highlights.

Apps
If you'd like the freedom of going paperless, check out these apps that can keep track of tickets (or points, as some of the apps call them) without your having to create and carry around tickets.

> ➤ *TeamSnap*
> This app was originally created to help parents keep track of their kids' sporting activities, but it also has a method of keeping track of babysitting co-ops. TeamSnap offers a free version, but you'll probably find that the features included in the Basic and Premium versions are very desirable for your co-op. Then you have to have a conversation with the rest of your co-op members to decide if the price is worth it. For more information about TeamSnap, visit www.teamsnap.com.

> ➤ *uSit iSit*
> Created especially for babysitting co-ops, this app allows your group to set up a sitting schedule, request a sitter, and keep track of points. With one tap, everyone in the group can know if a shift is available or full. You may find that your meetings are significantly shorter when you use a scheduling app like uSit iSit. For more information about this app, see usitisit.com or visit our blog for an exclusive interview with Steve Ingkavet, the creator of the uSit iSit app.

In addition to our internet resources, we've included some templates on the following pages to help you through your initial start-up meetings. You'll find an agenda to keep your meeting on track and forms for keeping the co-op kids' medical, emergency, and allergy information organized.

Babysitting Co-op Start-up Agenda

Co-op Leader:_____

Date:_____

Remind members to bring their Contact List information, Medical Release information and personal schedules with them prior to the meeting. Make it a point to invite the co-op members to voice any questions or concerns at the end of each point on the agenda.

Understand the Co-op Concepts
Take a moment to review the following key concepts.

- *Babysitting Co-ops*
  - ➢ What is a co-op and how does it work? (Defined on page 3)
  - ➢ What are the benefits of babysitting co-ops? (See page 4)

- *Principles of Successful Babysitting Co-ops*
  - ➢ Briefly touch on the Principles of Success (See pages 39-44)

- *Role of the Co-op Leader*
  - ➢ Touch on the role/responsibilities of the Co-op Leader (See pages 14-18)

Pulling it All Together
Now that everyone understands the general concepts, let's pull your program together.

Ticket Exchange
- ➢ Review the concept of the co-op tickets (See page 19).
- ➢ Pass the book around and show the co-op members what the tickets will look like once they're produced (See page 106).
- ➢ Identify the number of tickets each participant needs and jot this information down on the following page. Review *Start-up Tickets* examples if needed (See page 20).
- ➢ Turn to page 21 and review the *Payment of Tickets* examples which show how tickets are to be exchanged.
- ➢ Take a moment to role play a few ticket exchange.
- ➢ Discuss the concepts of *Rounding up Your Payment, Replacing Lost Tickets, Returning Co-op Tickets* and the importance of *Keep Those Tickets Moving* (See pages 23-26).

Name & Quantity of Tickets	**Name & Quantity of Tickets**

- *Calendaring*
  - ➢ Make a copy of the Small Group and Large Group sample calendars found on pages 34 and 36 for each co-op member prior to your meeting.
  - ➢ Discuss what a babysitting shift is and explain how shifts will repeat themselves throughout the calendar (See pages 28-30).
  - ➢ Pass out the two sample calendars and take a moment to identify whether you'll be functioning as a Small or Large co-op group. This sample calendar also effectively shows how shifts coordinate, overlap and repeat during the course of a month.
  - ➢ Ask each parent to choose a shift and then note these shifts on a white board or poster board.
  - ➢ Be sure to note holidays, school breaks, or special events as you're discussing your upcoming calendar.
  - ➢ Invite the co-op members to break into groups based on the day of their shift. They now can fill in their shifts on the provided blank calendars.
  - ➢ Discuss the following
    - ▪ How to schedule babysitting
    - ▪ *The 30-Minute Rule*
    - ▪ Switching shifts and the importance of timely notification
    - ▪ Canceling a shift only as a last resort
  - ➢ Schedule a time six to eight weeks out to assess the program. Set a second date toward the end of your calendaring period for planning your next calendaring segment. Note this on the master co-op calendar.

- *Establishing Rules*
  - ➢ Discuss why establishing rules is a necessary part of co-op.
  - ➢ Go through the rules, emphasizing the points that are most important for your group (starting on page 47). Have someone follow along in the book noting any rule alterations on a separate sheet of paper.

➤ Discuss the importance of creating a safe environment. Review the points that are applicable from Chapter Seventeen, Babyproofing, First Aid & Safety Tips (starting on page 129).

- *Expectant Mothers*
  - ➤ If applicable, discuss points in Chapter Eight (See page 57).
  - ➤ These same principles can apply toward co-op members who may need to take time off due to unexpected family circumstances.

- *Staying Connected*
  - ➤ Invite someone to coordinate a few social events.
  - ➤ Choose one or two activities that appeal to your group and schedule them on the calendar while at this meeting.
  - ➤ Review the suggested activities in Chapter Nine, Staying Connected in the Co-op (starting on page 61).

- *Weekend Co-op*
  Explain the differences between the Weekend Ticket Method (See details starting on page 73) and the Date Night Rotation Method (See details starting on page 77).
  - ➤ Decide whether you'll be using a weekend co-op and then choose the method that works best as outlined in Chapter Ten.
  - ➤ If you've chosen to use the Weekend Ticket Method, explain that a new set of tickets will be created and rotated only amongst the weekend co-op members. This method is an extension of the daytime co-op program and can only be used by those who are also willing to provide babysitting during the weekend hours.
  - ➤ Note the weekend participants and the number of tickets needed in the space on the following page.
  - ➤ If you've chosen to use the Date Night Rotation Method, explain that tickets are not necessary and that the group will operate per a set schedule. The calendar will be the main tool used for tracking this weekend schedule.
  - ➤ Both programs fill the same need and can be used independent of the daytime co-op program.
  - ➤ Fill in the weekend shifts on the master calendar as they apply to either the Weekend Ticket Method or the Date Night Rotation Method.

Name & Quantity of Tickets	**Name & Quantity of Tickets**

- *Part Two - Resources*
  - ➤ Invite the co-op members to ask any questions which may not have already been addressed.
  - ➤ Note the additional material found in the *Part Two - Resources* portion of this book if desired.
  - ➤ Feel free to touch quickly upon the title headings for the benefit of the entire group saving some time to explore these additional topics.
    - *Frequently Asked Questions* (See page 93)
    - *Online Resources, Apps & Forms* (Starting on page 97)
    - *Activities Kids Love* (See page 108)
    - *Healthy Snacks* (See page 121)
    - *Babyproofing, First Aid & Safety Tips* (See page 129)
    - *Ideas for Evening Activities, Dinners & Movies* (See page 141)

Contact Information Sheet

Name_____

Home Phone_____

Cell Phone_____

Work Phone_____

Address_____

_____

Email_____

Emergency Contact & Phone_____

_____

Children's Names/Ages:

_____

_____

_____

_____

Special Notes/Food Allergies_____

_____

Port-a-Crib Available: Yes/No

Weekend Co-op Participant: Yes/No

Medical Release Form

I _____, Parent or Legal Guardian of:

Child's Name_____ Date of Birth_____
Child's Name_____ Date of Birth_____
Child's Name_____ Date of Birth_____
Child's Name_____ Date of Birth_____

who is a minor child, hereby authorize any emergency medical or surgical treatment that may be necessary in my absence. I hereby authorize the attending physician, treatment center, or hospital to contact my insurance company on behalf of this minor child and agree to accept responsibility for any medical costs which may result from treatment.

Medical History
Child's Name/Allergies_____
Child's Name/Current Medications_____

Important Notes:
_____
_____
_____

Child's Physician_____ Phone_____
Insurance Co._____ ID #_____

Parent Information
Mother's Name_____
Home Phone_____ Work Phone_____ Cell Phone_____

Father's Name_____
Home Phone_____ Work Phone_____ Cell Phone_____

Emergency Contact
Name_____
Home Phone_____ Work Phone_____ Cell Phone_____
Relationship to Child_____

Parent/Guardian's Signature_____
Date_____

Babysitting Co-op Calendar

Month_____

Sunday	Monday	Tuesday	Wednesday	Thursday	Friday	Saturday

~~~
**1 Hour Ticket**
~~~

~~~
**1 Hour Ticket**
~~~

~~~
**1 Hour Ticket**
~~~

~~~
**1 Hour Ticket**
~~~

~~~
**1 Hour Ticket**
~~~

~~~
**1 Hour Ticket**
~~~

~~~
**1/2 Hour Ticket**
~~~

~~~
**1/2 Hour Ticket**
~~~

~~~
**1/2 Hour Ticket**
~~~

~~~
**1/2 Hour Ticket**
~~~

Weekend Co-op **1 Hour Ticket** Weekend Co-op	Weekend Co-op **1 Hour Ticket** Weekend Co-op
Weekend Co-op **1 Hour Ticket** Weekend Co-op	Weekend Co-op **1 Hour Ticket** Weekend Co-op
Weekend Co-op **1 Hour Ticket** Weekend Co-op	Weekend Co-op **1 Hour Ticket** Weekend Co-op
Weekend Co-op **1/2 Hour Ticket** Weekend Co-op	Weekend Co-op **1/2 Hour Ticket** Weekend Co-op
Weekend Co-op **1/2 Hour Ticket** Weekend Co-op	Weekend Co-op **1/2 Hour Ticket** Weekend Co-op

CHAPTER 15
ACTIVITIES KIDS LOVE

Most days, the children you're watching will have a wonderful time together. They'll enjoy making up games and peacefully playing with the toys or running around outside in a cheerful game of tag. But other days, they won't think of a single thing to do. "I'm bored," they'll say again and again, and they'll ask you for something to do.

It's tempting on days such as these to turn on a movie and watch them hypnotically plant themselves 15 inches away from the television set, suddenly quiet and absorbed. But we all know it's not good for them, and it can even be unnerving to watch their impassive faces stare at the screen.

When you're planning your co-op rules, it's a good idea to touch on television time. Even if TV is okay with everyone, it's still good to have some activities on hand, ready to pull out if the kids need a diversion. Here are some TV-free activities for you to try when it's your co-op day with the kids. We've divided these activities by type: Arts & Crafts (for you ambitious types), Creativity, Rainy Day, and Outdoor.

Finally, at the end of this chapter, we've listed some great resource books just in case you need more ideas. Take advantage of your local library. They're full of entertaining books, so check them out.

Arts & Crafts

Body Trace. Have each child lie down on a large piece of paper, like butcher paper or unprinted newsprint. Trace around the child's body and then allow him to add the details: facial features, clothing, etc. This can become a fun outdoor activity when you use sidewalk chalk. When you do it outside, the kids can create a whole scene of people on the driveway.

Box Car. For this craft, all you really need is a box big enough for a child to sit in, some markers or crayons, and four paper plates. Let them decorate the box to resemble a car, with the paper plates glued or stapled onto the outside for wheels. The great thing about this craft is that after the car is completed, the more energetic children can push the less energetic children around.

Crayon Copy Machine. This craft takes a bit of endurance, so it may not be a great activity for preschoolers, but young elementary school kids think it's great. Have them completely fill in one paper with crayon, a good heavy shiny coat of crayon wax. Then have them put a clean sheet of paper in front of themselves with the crayoned paper face down on top of the clean sheet. Next, encourage them to draw a picture with a pencil on top of the wax-covered sheet that is laying face down. When they peel back the top paper, they have an exact duplicate of their drawing in crayon on the bottom sheet. Neat!

Crayon Rubbings. Tell the kids to look through the house or yard for small, textured objects such as quarters, leaves, keys, and bottle caps. Once they have a collection, tell them to arrange it on the table and then put a sheet of paper over it. Then, using the long side of a crayon, rub right over the objects.

Bird Feeder. You'll need yarn, a pinecone for each child, peanut butter, and birdseed. Let the kids try to spread peanut butter on the pinecone. While this process is messy, it sure is entertaining to watch. Just make sure they don't put their plastic knives back in the peanut butter after they lick it, as they inevitably will. Then you can let them roll the sticky, prickly pinecone in a plate of birdseed before you hang it (with the string) from a tree near the window.

Fall Crowns and Bracelets. In the fall, have the kids collect a whole bag of leaves in the yard. Tell them it's a game and they won't realize that they're actually doing one of your chores. Then string the leaves onto pipe cleaners and shape them into crowns and bracelets.

Macaroni Cards. Make simple cards out of heavy paper or poster board. Then let the kids glue macaroni or other dry pasta to the fronts of the cards. This might be a fun activity to do when someone in the co-op has a birthday.

Oven Clay. Have the kids mix 4 cups of flour, 1 cup of salt and 1 ¾ cups of water. When the dough has a nice even texture, roll the dough out and let the kids cut shapes with cookie cutters. If they're making ornaments or something else they'd like to hang, remind them to make a little hole in the top. Bake their creations on a cookie sheet at 200 degrees for about three hours. Once they've cooled, the kids can use poster paints or tempera paints to decorate them. These make great Christmas ornaments.

Paper Bag Masks. Kids sure do love dressing up, but Halloween only comes once a year. Next time you go to the grocery store ask for paper instead of plastic so you'll have a good stock of big paper sacks. Cut holes for the kids' eyes and let them decorate the rest of the bag with markers or paints or crayons. Give them some ideas: tiger, robot, princess, elephant, or a chicken.

Paper Dolls. Get on Google and do a search for "Print Paper Dolls." You'll get hundreds or results. Just print a bunch of dolls and clothes from the Internet and then supply the kids with crayons and colored pencils to color their dolls and their stylish wardrobes. You may need to help cut them out. If you want to make them more durable, glue the dolls to poster board before cutting them out. When they're finished, give each child an envelope or gallon-size Zip-loc bag to keep their creations safe.

Placemats. Give each child a placemat-sized piece of poster board. Then let them decorate the placemat with glitter, stickers, dried flowers or leaves, drawings, or whatever else they like. To create a durable surface, you'll want to cover the placemats with contact paper. Keep the placemats at your house, and whenever the kids come over, they can eat their snack or lunch at their own placemat. This can cut down on arguments over who sits where.

Paper Chains. We like to make paper chains for counting down days to a much-anticipated event such as Christmas, the neighborhood block party or upcoming birthday party. Cut strips of construction paper in various colors and then have the kids string them together in loops. If you use glue, kids can do it on their own but they may get frustrated and quit. It's best to use a stapler. Have the children string them through and then you staple them together.

Pet Rocks. This is a two-part activity because first you have to go find the perfect rocks and then you have to decorate them. They can be decorated with googly eyes, pom poms, fun fur for hair, mustaches or beards, pebbles for ears, noses, and chins. You get the idea.

Play Dough. This is a great play dough recipe. It's nice and soft and can stay good in your refrigerator for up to one year. Play dough is a great way to help children refine their small motor skills while creating a soothing effect because they're working with their hands.

Recipe:
3 cups flour
3 cups water
1 Tablespoon cream of tartar
3-5 drops of food coloring

1 ½ cups salt
2 Tablespoons cooking oil

Directions:
Cook the mixture slowly at medium high heat, stirring constantly until the dough pulls away from the sides of the pan and you can't stir it any longer (this is a good workout; you can let your hand weights gather dust today!). When it cools enough to touch, knead it for 3 or 4 minutes until it's nice and smooth. When you pass it out to the kids, make sure to also give them some interesting kitchen utensils or cookie cutters. Our kids like to use a pie trimmer, plastic baby forks, and especially the garlic press. Store it in a resealable sandwich bag in the fridge.

Sewing Cards. Draw pictures on lightweight cardboard. Then use a hole punch to put holes at the angles or corners of the pictures. Next, cut lengths of yarn and tightly wrap tape around the ends to make a "needle." The kids can pull the yarn in and out of the holes to sew a picture. Younger children may need help to understand the process. This is great practice for kids who need help with their fine motor skills.

Shoe Box Guitar. With your adult scissors, cut a 2 ½" hole in the lid of a shoebox. Put the lid on the box and then let the kids string rubber bands around the box, lining them up over the hole. Then let the beautiful racket begin!

Creativity

Blindfold Guide. You barely get the blindfold on before she starts giggling. We're not sure why that is, but they sure do like this game. One person wears the blindfold and another is the guide. The guide takes the blindfolded person around the house, handing objects to her or having her smell things. The blindfolded person has to try and figure out what they're holding or smelling. If you're brave enough, wear the blindfold yourself. This is sure to please them.

Biggest and Smallest. Have the kids search the house for objects in the same category: books, for example. Then they have to find the biggest and smallest in that category. If you have any kids in the group who are learning to write, have them write down their findings. They can even trace the biggest and smallest objects onto the paper for a more scientific reading of their data. Some other good objects are pots and pans, houseplants, socks, and pencils.

Crazy Kazoos. Give each child a cardboard tube. Let the children decorate their tubes with stickers, markers, glitter, and construction paper. Then punch three holes in a line toward the top of the tube. Cover the opposite end with a piece of wax paper and secure it with a rubber band. Turn on some fast-paced marching music or children's songs and let them form a marching band.

The Day I Was Born. There's nothing kids love more than hearing about their own births. With this activity, kids can create the story themselves—even if it is a bit fictional. Rachel's oldest daughter wrote in her book that the mom and dad and brand new baby went to London and the mother rented a stroller while the father looked for a job. It sounds lovely and romantic, but it didn't happen. That's okay. Let the kids write their own birth stories and then staple the pages together in a book. Then read them all in a grand story time. They'll pay attention like they never have before.

Dinosaur Bone Hunt. Budding archaeologists will have a good time with this one. Get a bunch of Popsicle sticks and hide them. Indoors, you can hide them in the sofa cushions, behind pillows, on windows sills, etc. Outdoors, put them in loose soil about an inch below the surface. Then provide them with sophisticated digging tools—like spoons—and have them dig for bones. After they find them, they can brush the dirt and dust off with an old toothbrush. If you give them some glue, they can reconstruct the complete dinosaur out of the bones.

Emergency Room. Supplies: a tape measure, a small flashlight, a scale, an ace bandage and maybe a few band-aids for good measure. Concocting dramatic situations is pretty easy for kids, but now they get to fix them as well. They can weigh and measure their patients, wrap up a hurt leg, look in their eyes and ears with the flashlight and give plenty of good advice.

Guess That Animal. This is the most basic of charades. Children take turns pretending to be an animal and the rest of them guess what it is. Everyone is happiest when sound effects are allowed and even encouraged.

Mailbox. Receiving a letter in the mail is about as exciting as it gets for little kids, but it doesn't happen very often. Obtain an old mailbox or make one out of a shoebox. Then give the kids supplies for making letters for each other, complete with stickers for stamps. Let them take turns delivering and receiving the mail throughout the afternoon.

Pantomime. Explain that actors in a pantomime show do not talk. They act out a story by using their hands and face and body movements only. Demonstrate a pantomime for them by being a person who has lost something. You can look all over the room, under things, in your pockets, even under the kids' hair or in their ears. Make sure you look very concerned and sad about not finding it. When they're done laughing at your mime show, encourage them to make up their own. Then they can perform for each other and to music if you prefer.

Paper Snowflakes. Fold a piece of plain white paper into fourths or fifths or sixths. Then, with childproof scissors, have the children cut shapes out of the sides and ends of their folded snowflakes. Unfolding the snowflakes is always a fun surprise. These make great window decorations for December.

Pizza Delivery. Working at a place that delivers pizza would be the ultimate in fun for kids, wouldn't it? So let them give it a try. You'll need a box for the oven, which they can decorate with markers for the knobs and lights and buttons, cookie sheets for baking the play dough pizzas, egg noodles for the cheese, buttons for the pepperoni, a phone for incoming orders, and a pad of paper to write down the order and the address, and a box for delivery. Pretend to call the pizza place. One of the kids answers the phone and takes your order. Mix up some of that great homemade play dough (See page 111). Help the kids roll the play dough out into a big circle on the cookie sheet. Then they can decorate it with dry egg noodles for cheese and buttons for pepperoni. They bake it in their oven and then deliver it to you. You decide on whether or not they deserve a tip. Let the kids take turns ordering the pizza after you have yours.

What Am I Drawing? This is another fun guessing game, however, doesn't work well with toddlers. Children preschool age and older think it's fun, especially if there's a chalkboard or whiteboard available. Divide the kids into teams (boys vs. girls isn't really fair with this game until kids are in about 2nd grade). Whisper a word into the ear of one of the children and she draws it for the others, but only her own team guesses. If they guess right, they get a point. If they can't get it, the other team can guess and earns a point.

Outdoor Fun

Bicycle Wash. A junior version of a car wash: drag all the bikes out and give the kids buckets of warm, soapy water, spray bottles, rags, and towels, but make sure the kids you're babysitting have extra clothes or a swimsuit for this activity.

Bubbles. Here's the recipe for out-of-sight bubbles:

> 3 cups water
> 1 cup dishwashing liquid (Joy and Dawn are rumored to produce the best bubbles)
> 1/3 cup light corn syrup
>
> Make some homemade bubble wands out of coat hangers, paper clips, hula-hoops, or flyswatters.

Cloud Watching. This activity can be just the thing to calm down overtired, grumpy kids. Take them outside and make them lie on their backs with their little hands behind their heads. If you're energetic, you could get a blanket for everyone to lie on. If not, don't worry about it—they're kids. Point out a penguin in the sky and it won't be long before they're all excitedly pointing out flowers, boats and other imaginative objects in the sky.

Four Square. Still the best darn game at recess, even after all these years. All you need is a red playground ball and some sidewalk chalk. For smaller kids, just have them bounce and catch it in their squares. This will be plenty considering their skill level. When they're bigger and get the hang of it, the server (in square one, you'll remember) can call out crazy variations: bus stop, fire alarm, mailbox, big tomato, around the world colors, and last but not least, Normal.

Fox and Goose. It's too bad you can't play this game every day; you have to wait for snow. Stomp out a 10 to 20 ft. (in diameter) circle in the yard or driveway. Then stomp out dividing lines across the circle, pie fashion. Your big pie should have eight pieces. The goose begins in the middle of the circle, and the fox begins somewhere on the perimeter. The fox has to chase down the goose, but the trick is that both animals have to stay on the paths—no cutting across allowed. When the goose is caught, they switch roles, or if you have a crowd waiting on the sidelines, let a new fox and goose play.

Lemonade Stand. Lemonade stands have kept our children busy for hours. There's the promise of cold hard cash, the friendliest of customers, and all-you-can drink lemonade. This is a great chance to teach about money, making change, and a little lesson in manners is usually in order as well.

Hopscotch. You'll need to draw the first hopscotch and show them how it's done. After that, the kids are all ambition and will probably draw hopscotch with 746 squares in it, all the way up the street. Hopping is sure to wear them out.

Quarter Journeys. Set out on a walk on a nice day with a quarter. When you get to a crossroads, flip the quarter. If it's heads, turn right. If it's tails, turn left. Continue straight until you get to the next corner, then flip again. For some reason, the prospect of the unknown is very exciting. Just make sure you don't get lost.

Rock Hunt. If you've taken a two-year-old for a walk, you know how often they stop to look at things on the ground. Maybe it's because they're so close to the ground. In any case, an outing designed solely for the purpose of looking at and collecting rocks is ideal for toddlers. Give them each a container for their rock treasures. Like any hunter, the kids will want to inspect their treasures when they return. You can even fill a dishpan with water and let them wash them before they sort and examine them.

Sidewalk Chalk. Not only is sidewalk chalk inexpensive, but you can send their artistic endeavors outside—no cleanup. If they have trouble thinking of something to draw, suggest that they draw a family picture, a self-portrait, or their favorite animals. They can draw roads for their Hot Wheels cars with houses and garages, their school and church, and even the giant parking lot at the grocery store.

Spring Patrol. As you're despairing that winter will never end, send the kids out on Spring Patrol to look for signs of new life. They can inspect the shrubs and trees for bulging buds; scrape away some old dry grass to look for the spring green beneath. Tell them to remember to listen: maybe they'll hear some baby birds or insects chirping. For older kids, send them out with a notebook to document their findings. They can even bring some specimens inside to glue in their notebooks.

Three-Legged Relay Race. This is the old game we all looked forward to on Field Day at school each year. Using a bandana or rag, tie a right leg from one child to a left leg from another child. Or you could be a good sport and tie a child to yourself. Then run around, make an obstacle course to navigate, or see if they can run through an oscillating sprinkler without getting soaked.

Trash Brigade. Give each child a pair of latex gloves and a trash bag. Then take them for a walk and have them pick up every single piece of trash they can see. If you live near a park, clean up the park. Some kids think this is not such a great activity, and in that case you'll need an incentive, like homemade cookies when you get home or a jellybean for each piece of trash they put in their bags. Not only will you be doing your community a favor, but it may make these "adults in training" think twice before littering in the future.

Wheelbarrow Moving Van. This "game" can be very handy if you have some real work to be done. Let's say, for example, you need to move some rocks from one part of the yard to the other. Tell the kids you're moving, and you need them to load the van. They put the rocks in the wheelbarrow and then you can all help out when you cross town (the yard) and unload at the new house.

Rainy Day

Balloon Volleyball. Make a net by stringing yarn between two chairs in the family room. Divide the kids in two teams and give them a balloon. They hit it back and forth across the net, trying to keep it off the floor. They earn a point when the other team lets it fall on their side of the net. Play until one team reaches ten points and wins the game.

Box Train. Line up as many boxes as you have and make believe it's a train. Hopefully the kids can each have their own "box car." If you have a bell, hand it to the child in the front. They can take turns being the conductor and yelling "All Aboard!" Choose new conductors until everyone has had a turn.

Dress Ups. Pack an old suitcase with dress-ups and disguises for rainy days. Look through your closet and don't forget the thrift store. Here are some ideas: fancy old dresses, scarves, purses, hats, a feather boa, a cape, shoes of all kinds, a bathrobe, wigs and fake fur for beards, a bandanna, costume jewelry, glasses or sunglasses, wands, a tiara, angel wings, a tutu or two, neckties, and silk flowers.

Flannel Board Stories. Flannel board stories will take some serious preparation on your part, but children love them. Visit the children's reference section in your library and ask for books containing flannel board stories. These books have everything in them you need to create your own flannel board and stories. They have templates for the cutouts and the stories as well. After you've prepared the stories, sit the kids down in front of you like you're the library lady at story time and tell the story—maybe two or three times. Then let them take turns telling the story and moving the figures on the flannel board.

Forts. Drag some of your kitchen chairs into a room with a big, empty space. Then drape blankets over the chairs until there isn't any light peeping through. Supply the kids with a flashlight and watch their imaginations come to life. All of the sudden this very simple structure will become a secret hideout, a castle or base camp for those overly active little boys.

Hot & Cold. Choose an object for the children to hide and find. Have one child leave the room. While he's gone, another child will hide the object. Then call the seeker back into the room and tell him to start looking for the object. When he's close to it, the children will say "Hot," but when he's far away they'll say "Cold." Of course, they'll come up with silly things to say like, "Ouch! It's burning! It's so hot!" and that's part of the fun. Another version of this game is to have the kids sing a song while the seeker looks for the object. When he's close, they sing louder, and when he's far away they sing softly.

Jack-in-the-Box Pop-up Game. A moving box is perfect. Let one child sit in the box with the flaps loosely closed. The others skip around the outside singing "Pop Goes the Weasel," or this little ditty our own kids made up: "Jack in the box, Jack in the box, Jack in the box, POP UP!" When the kid in the box pops up, they all roar with laughter and shout, "Do it again!"

Mix-and-Match. Give a child a muffin tin and then let her sort objects into the muffin cups. This is great practice for sorting and classifying and also for fine motor skills. Items for sorting could include Lego blocks, puzzle pieces, plastic army men, clothes pins, crayons, baby bottle rings, paper clips, and dry beans.

Music-Stop-Squat. In this game each player must stop and squat—fast. Play some fun music and have everyone march around the room in time to the music. Assign one child to be the spotter. Stop the music! Everyone must squat. The last one to squat is out of the game. He must become the spotter and catch the last squatter in the next round.

Noodle Jewelry and Button Rings. String hollow, dry noodles onto a string or some colorful yarn. For the button rings, thread pipe cleaners through the buttonholes and then shape the pipe cleaners into rings. The button is the jewel on top. Of course, noodle jewelry is fragile, so you better make a jewelry shoebox to store it in.

Silly Olympics. Have the kids brainstorm silly Olympic events. Place a masking tape starting line and finish line on the floor for your silly races. Here are some examples of silly races: get from the starting line to the finish line with one hand in the air and the other one on the ground, walk backwards while flapping your arms, crawl on all fours while balancing a book on your head, or hopping on one foot.

Sleeping, Sleeping. This activity has an ulterior motive (it forces them to lie down), but kids love it nonetheless. Have all the kids lie down and pretend to be asleep. Ahh, isn't that nice? Then you say "Sleeping, sleeping, Everybody sleeping, Sleeping, sleeping, time for lights out. When we wake up we're going to be _____" (fill in the blank with animals, inanimate objects, trains, fairies, flowers, etc.). Then you say "Good morning!" and they all jump up, pretending to be whatever it is you suggested. As soon as you say "Sleeping, sleeping" they have to get back down and pretend to sleep again. Kids like to decide what to be, so let them take turns leading.

Story Time. Here's a list of great read-aloud books for rainy days:

Chicka Chicka ABC by Bill Martin Jr. and John Archambault
Curious George by H.A. Rey
Blueberries for Sal by Robert McCloskey
Bubba the Cowboy Prince: A Fractured Texas Tale by Helen Ketteman
Cloudy With a Chance of Meatballs by Judi Barrett
The Cow that Laid an Egg by Andy Cutbill
Frog and Toad Are Friends by Arnold Lobel
Goodnight, Goodnight, Construction Site by Sherri Duskey Rinker
King Bidgood's in the Bathtub by Audrey Wood
Llama Llama Time to Share by Anna Dewdney
Kumak's Fish by Michael Bania
Make Way for Ducklings by Robert McCloskey
Mike Mulligan and the Steam Shovel by Virginia Lee Burton
My Cat, the Silliest Cat in the World by Gilles Bachelet
My Father the Dog by Elizabeth Bluemle
Nightsong by Ari Berk
Oh No! Not Again! by Mac Barnett and Dan Santat
The Princess Mouse by Aaron Shepard
The School Mouse by Dick King-Smith
Starry Safari by Linda Ashman
Stone Soup, An Old Tale retold by Marcia Brown
Tikki Tikki Tembo by Arlene Mosel
Too Many Toys by David Shannon
The Very Hungry Caterpillar by Eric Carle
A Visitor for Bear by Bonny Becker
Where the Wild Things Are by Maurice Sendak

CHAPTER 16
HEALTHY SNACKS

At your first meeting, you probably discussed rules for food and snack time. Some mothers care very much about what their children eat and some are more relaxed in this area. It may be difficult to come to a consensus about something as personal as nutrition, but we've included snack ideas and recipes in this chapter that we think most mothers would be okay with.

We're leaving out snacks with a high sugar or fat content because we don't like picking our children up at 11:30 in the morning and finding out that they just ate two chocolate cupcakes. There goes lunch. And sugary snacks are not so great for the babysitter either.

Let's do a simple math equation. You're watching six children and you give each child three chocolate chip cookies at 2:00 in the afternoon. What do you get? You get six very crabby kids at 2:45 pm, but it's still an hour and fifteen minutes until their parents come to pick them up.

Some of the snack ideas in this chapter require little or no preparation; some require some preparation on your part. Others can be made with the help of children. If you can manage to pull kitchen chairs up to your counter, be brave and let the kids help you in the kitchen. Don't forget to have them wash their hands. Research shows that when a child prepares her own snack she is 78% more likely to eat it than if her mother prepares it. No kidding.

We've divided this chapter into three sections:
- Quick and Easy
- Worth the Work
- Kid Participant Worthy

We wish you many happy snack times.

Quick and Easy

Bagels and Cream Cheese. If you can find the little appetizer bagels that come in a big bag, don't pass them up. There are usually too many in a bag for one family to eat before they go stale, but they freeze well so take out what you need and freeze the rest. Kids love small foods, and those little bagels are irresistibly cute. Just slice them in half, spread some cream cheese on them and serve them up.

Quesadillas. Warm a skillet or griddle. Spread butter or margarine on one side of a tortilla. Place the tortilla, butter side down, on the griddle, and then cover the tortilla with grated cheese. Butter another tortilla and place it, butter side up, on top of the cheese. When the cheese looks melted, flip the whole thing over and watch it so it doesn't burn. Then remove it from the griddle, slice it up pizza-style and serve it to the kids.

Veggies and Peanut Butter. Slice up carrots and celery and serve them with peanut butter. If you spread the peanut butter into the middle of the celery stick and put raisins on top you'll have the famous "Ants on a Log" snack. We personally haven't had too much luck getting kids to eat "Ants on a Log," but if you succeed, email us and tell us your secret.

Edamame. It's just a fancy name for soybeans in the pod. We mentioned these in the date night dinner section as well because kids really like them and they're nutritious. You can find them in the freezer section. Just follow the directions on the package. Usually, you just boil them or microwave them for a few minutes and, presto, they're ready. Super easy.

Hard-boiled Eggs. If you oversee them, you can let the kids crack and roll the eggs before they peel the shell off. This is a fun activity for them, but you'll probably want to rinse them off afterward so the little tiny shell pieces can get washed off. For very small kids, mash the egg up with a fork and let them eat it with a spoon. A little salt and pepper are in order.

Cheese Cubes. Cut cheese up into cubes and serve them on little dishes. Varieties to try include the ever-popular Cheddar, Colby, Colby-Jack, Mozzarella, and Monterrey Jack, and Swiss. Apple slices are a great companion to cheese cubes.

Worth the Work

Fruited Yogurt Dip. *This dip is an incentive to eat fresh fruit.*
1 (8 oz.) package cream cheese
2 (8 oz.) cartons orange yogurt
2 Tbs. brown sugar
1 tsp. lemon juice
1 (8 oz.) can crushed pineapple
¾ cup flaked coconut

Beat cream cheese at medium speed with an electric mixer until fluffy. Add the next three ingredients and beat until smooth. Stir in pineapple and coconut. Serve with fresh fruit. Refrigerate any leftovers.

Fruit Jello. *This one is especially good for babies and toddlers.*
¼ cup cold water
1 package unflavored gelatin
½ cup boiling water
1 cup fruit juice
1 cup fruit puree

Put cold water in a bowl and sprinkle gelatin on top to swell. Add boiling water to dissolve gelatin. Add fruit juice and puree. Mix well. Pour into ice cube trays or other containers and refrigerate until set.

Chocolate Yogurt Popsicles
1 cup plain yogurt
3 Tbs. light corn syrup
2 Tbs. chocolate syrup
½ tsp. vanilla
2/3 cup milk

Use a fork to stir together the yogurt and corn syrup. Add the chocolate syrup and vanilla and stir until combined. Add the milk and mix well. Pour mixture into 8 (6 oz.) ice-pop molds or paper cups, filling each about ¾ full. Cover the molds with lids or the paper cups with foil. Insert the sticks (use wooden ice-pop sticks if using paper cups). Freeze until solid. To serve, peel away the paper from the paper cups. Makes 8.

Peanut Butter Muffins
2 eggs
1 cup milk
1 banana, mashed
¼ cup peanut butter
1/3 cup vegetable oil
¼ cup frozen apple juice concentrate, thawed
¼ cup nonfat dry milk
2 ¼ cup flour
1 ½ tsp. baking powder
1 tsp. baking soda
Nonstick spray

Preheat oven to 350 degrees. In a small bowl, break the eggs and use a fork to beat them a little bit. In a large bowl, combine the milk, mashed banana, peanut butter, vegetable oil, apple juice, dry milk, and the eggs from the small bowl. Mix with a mixing spoon until the mixture is creamy. Add the flour, baking powder, and the baking soda into the large bowl. Mix again. Line a muffin tin with paper liners or lightly spray with nonstick spray. Spoon the muffin mix carefully. Fill each muffin cup about 2/3 full. Bake for 12-15 minutes. Remove from muffin tin and cool on wire rack.

Cinnamuffins
¼ cup oil
½ cup dark molasses
1 cup applesauce
1 ½ cup whole wheat flour
½ tsp. baking soda
1 ½ tsp. baking powder
¾ tsp. cinnamon
Pinch cloves
½ tsp. salt
½ cup raisins

Preheat oven to 375 degrees. Coat a 12-muffin tin with nonstick spray. Mix oil, molasses, and applesauce. Sift together the dry ingredients. Stir together wet and dry ingredients and raisins. Drop into muffin cups and bake 18-20 minutes. Cool on wire rack.

Kid Participant Worthy

Smoothies. We feel like we need to put a disclaimer in the smoothie section because children and blenders don't seem to go together. But if you're careful, and make sure the lid is on before they start pushing buttons, we think everything should turn out fine. Kids love the plopping noise the fruit makes when they drop it into the blender. But nothing beats the power they feel when they push a button and the kitchen is suddenly deafeningly loud. There's nothing like it to a four-year-old boy. We find that smoothies are a hit because they resemble milkshakes but they have real bona fide fruit in them (you just can't see it after it's been pulverized). Here are some of our favorite smoothie recipes. For each recipe, just put all the stuff in the blender and go wild with the buttons until it's, you know, smooth.

Berry Blast
1 cup Cran-Raspberry juice
1 (8 oz.) container vanilla yogurt
1 cup frozen unsweetened strawberries or raspberries
½ cup seedless grapes
3-4 tsp. sugar
3-4 ice cubes

Twin-Berry Yogurt Shake
2/3 cup frozen unsweetened strawberries
2/3 cup frozen vanilla yogurt
¾-1 cup cranberry juice cocktail

Yogurt Milkshake
1 cup vanilla yogurt
1 cup orange juice
1 ripe banana

Sunny Sipper
½ cup orange juice
3 Tbs. lemon juice
1 can (13 oz.) evaporated milk
1 can (13 oz.) apricot nectar

Tropical Blend
½ cup vanilla yogurt
½ cup crushed pineapple, undrained
¼ cup orange juice
½ peeled kiwi or banana
1 to 3 ice cubes

Triple Shake
1 cup each of 3 different fruits
5 ice cubes

Banana Smoothie
1 ½ cups milk
1 large banana
¼ tsp. vanilla
1 Tbs. peanut butter

Chili-Cheese Popcorn. *The trick to this snack is to add the Parmesan seasoning while the popcorn is still hot so the cheese will melt and stick to the popcorn. Use homemade air-popped popcorn because it has no added fat and also because standing around the air popper is a real treat for the kids. One time, Rachel's husband Ben thought it would be fun to leave the cover off the popper so it would spray the kids with popcorn. He certainly didn't suspect (or did he?) that the children thought it was the end of the world when popcorn went shooting all over the kitchen.*

14 cups hot air-popped popcorn
2 Tbs. grated Parmesan cheese
½ tsp. chili powder
¼ tsp. dried oregano or marjoram

While the popcorn is popping, in a custard cup, stir together the cheese, chili powder, and oregano or marjoram. Transfer the hot popcorn to a large bowl and quickly toss it with the cheese mixture. Serve immediately.

Caramel Apple Dippers. *Ever since McDonald's came out with their apple dippers, this one has been a hit. And older kids can make this if they know how to use the microwave and you slice up the apples. The following recipe makes only one serving.*

3 caramels cut into small pieces
1 Tbs. dark corn syrup
1 tsp. water
1 large apple, cored and sliced

In a medium microwave-safe bowl, stir together the caramels, corn syrup and water. Microwave these ingredients on high power for 30 seconds. Stir, then microwave for 15 seconds, or until the caramels are completely melted. Serve with the apple slices.

Awesome Applesauce. *As with the smoothies, let them push the buttons on the blender. But don't let them near the knife. Better yet, cut the apples up before your babysitting shift begins and then you'll feel like you're really prepared because all your ingredients are ready for you ahead of time.*

2 small red apples
2 Tbs. lemon juice
2 tsp. sugar
2 pinches cinnamon

Peel the apples and cut them in small pieces. Throw out the cores. Put the apples and lemon juice in the blender and blend until very smooth. Pour the mixture into small bowls and stir in the sugar and cinnamon.

Pretzels. *This is a big hit, but it can also be a big mess. Don't do it on a day when your energy reserves are low.*

1 Tbs. yeast
½ c. warm water
1 tsp. honey
1 1/3 c. flour (try half white flour and half whole wheat flour)
1 tsp. salt

Preheat oven to 325 degrees. Put the yeast in a small bowl with the water and honey. Stir a little, and then let it sit for 5 minutes. Mix the flour and salt together in a medium-sized bowl. Add yeast mixture to flour mixture. Stir everything together. Use a spoon to start but finish with your hands. The dough is ready when it's still a little crumbly and flaky. Put the dough on the cutting board and knead it like you're playing with clay. Divide it up among the kids and let them each knead their own piece. Then let them roll it out like a snake and shape it into a pretzel. Put the pretzels on a greased baking sheet and bake for about 10-12 minutes. Let them cool a little before the kids eat them.

CHAPTER 17
BABYPROOFING, FIRST AID & SAFETY TIPS

The days you hold co-op at your house can be wonderful days. Your children will have friends over to play with, so they're generally happy and busy. You can ensure that your co-op days will be more tranquil by arranging things in your home to avoid accidents, extra messes and spills.

Nothing can ruin a day quite like a trip to the emergency room, especially if you have to haul four other children along, besides the injured one. And, on a less consequential plane, nothing can put you in a fouler mood than having a bottle of bleach spilled on your new carpet.

Of course, with children, accidents will happen. But there is much you can do to avoid accident and injury. Unfortunately, homes can very be dangerous places for children if stairs are not blocked, poisons are not locked away, and furnishings have sharp corners.

This chapter will help you to make sure your home is a safe place for your kids and the kids you watch on co-op days. You'll find childproofing checklists by age, general safety tips and rules, and a first-aid section for those times when accidents can't be avoided.

Childproofing Checklists by Age

As a parent, you are well aware of safety hazards and how to protect your own children from them. Somehow, though, when your two-year-old becomes a three-year-old, you forget which dangers plagued him just one year earlier. And it's not until your first co-op day with your friend's two-year-old that you relearn that potted plants and two-year-olds do not mix.

Maybe we have very short memories, or maybe it's because our kids change gradually, or maybe it's just that we know our own kids so well that we know what to anticipate. All we know is that when you have other people's kids over, it's a really good idea to double-check your babyproofing.

So here's an age appropriate checklist of things you need to put up and out of the way. If you're having a two-year-old and a one-year-old over on your co-op day, check the one-year-old list to cover your bases. A thorough safety check could save you an unnecessary headache and it could also save your new carpet from all that potting soil.

Six Months
- ***Electrical Outlet Covers.*** Get down on your elbows to see what a crawling baby would find in his explorations. The most prominent wall features at this height are electrical outlets. Make sure each unused outlet has a plastic plug inserted in it. You can buy these at children's stores, discount stores, and even some grocery stores.
- ***Electrical Cords.*** Some babies will actually try chewing on electrical cords. Make sure cords are hidden behind furniture or wound up and secured instead of lying loose against the wall.
- ***Small Toys.*** Legos, Polly Pockets, and Barbie shoes are terribly interesting to babies but not so great for their digestive tracts.
- ***Coins.*** Keep your purse out of babies' reach because coins are small, shiny, and just the right size to get lodged in their windpipes.

Twelve Months
- ***Blind or Drapery Cords.*** Either tie up long cords or install cord shorteners on your blinds and drapes. Even after they're tied up, survey them from a child's point of view. Is there a sofa or

crib the child could climb up in order to reach the cord?

- **Lamps and Light Fixtures.** Make sure children can't reach any light bulbs, which could cause burns on their fingers.
- **Dresser Drawers.** For some reason, climbing into a dresser drawer is appealing to little ones. Make sure drawers are always closed, and if a dresser is susceptible to falling over, anchor it to the wall.
- **Fireplaces, Heaters, Wood-Burning Stoves, Furnaces, and Radiators.** When one of our kids was about this age she touched a wood burning stove at a friend's house and ended up with a blister on the end of each of her fingers. Put up some sort of grill or grate so kids can't get close enough to touch these items. And don't forget that most of these surfaces retain their heat long after the fire has died down or the heat has been turned off.
- **House Plants.** Keep them out of reach where children can't get into the dirt or eat the leaves. Be aware of which houseplants are poisonous and make sure children can't get near them. Poisonous plants include azalea, caladium, daffodil bulbs, Daphne, dumb can, English ivy, foxglove, holly, hyacinth bulbs, hydrangea, iris rootstalk, Japanese yew, Jerusalem cherry, larkspur, laurel, lily of the valley, mistletoe, narcissus bulbs, oleander, philodendron, privet, rhododendron, rhubarb leaves, sweet peas, tomato plant leaves, wisteria pods and seeds, and yew.
- **Stairs.** Put gates up to keep new walkers away from stairs. Gates can also be great for blocking off parts of the house that aren't childproofed.
- **Coffee Tables.** Kids this age love coffee tables because they're just the right height for walking around, but make sure corners are padded, and if you have a glass-topped table, cover it with a table pad. You never know when a Hot Wheels car will get slammed down on it, and you don't want little shards of glass flying around.
- **Knickknacks and Bookends.** Don't take chances leaving your beautiful things out on co-op day, and make sure that heavy objects are out of the way. Toddlers can be stronger than they look.
- **High Chairs.** Even if your own child doesn't use the safety strap, always use it with the co-op kids because they may rely on it to keep them upright.

Eighteen Months

- *Doors.* Around eighteen months, children discover the appeal of doors: you never know what's on the other side. We're assuming you don't want to spend your morning chasing children down the street, so it's a good idea to put a plastic door knob cover on all doors leading to places you don't want them to go.
- *Windows.* Above ground windows should have window guards on them to keep children from tumbling out.
- *Banisters, Railings, and Balconies.* Check to make sure that balusters (the upright posts) aren't loose and that they're less than 5 inches apart. If they're further apart than 5 inches, rig a temporary wall of plastic or firm mesh along the length of the balcony.
- *Tablecloths.* Toddlers will want to pull down the tablecloth to see what was on top of the table. Note: we said "was."
- *Scatter Rugs.* Make sure your rugs have non-skid backings and that they're not tripping hazards.
- *Wastebaskets.* Never put anything in an open wastebasket that you wouldn't mind the toddlers playing with—or eating.
- *Toilets.* If you're watching children this age, train yourself to keep the bathroom door closed. You don't want them playing in the toilet water.

Two Years

- *Exercise Equipment.* Treadmills are particularly interesting to two-year-olds. Make sure, if you have a treadmill out in the open, that it's unplugged. Free weights can be dropped on toes if they're accessible to little ones. And exercise bicycles, especially older ones, are a big danger to toddlers.
- *Standing Water.* Don't leave water in a bucket outside because a toddler can fall into it and not be able to get out. Also, never let a child go out to even a wading pool unless you are standing guard.
- *Matches.* Keep matches way out of reach.
- *Cleaning Solutions.* If you keep your cleaning solutions in a low cupboard, install a safety latch there. Your own children may be trained to stay away from such things, but other people's kids may not have the same boundaries.
- *Medicine Cabinet.* Keep medicines and vitamins in an inaccessible spot.
- *Balloons.* Balloons are the single most dangerous non-food

choking hazard for kids under three. Don't let small children attempt to blow up balloons, and if a balloon pops, quickly gather up the popped pieces and throw them away. Mylar balloons are safer for small children because they slowly deflate, rather than popping.

- *Plastic Bags.* Keep your plastic bags in a drawer or cupboard with a child safety latch installed on it.

Three Years

- *Step Stools.* Provide a safe step stool for children in the bathroom. Some three-year-olds are so small that they have a hard time getting up to the toilet. And almost all children this age need a boost to reach the faucets for washing their hands. You don't want them climbing in the bathroom.
- **Rope/Cording.** One of us recently discovered a jump rope around her three-year-olds' neck; another child was pulling the rope. The one with the rope around her neck was being the horse and the other child was leading her to the pasture. This is not good. It's best to put the ropes away.
- *Bunk Beds.* There's a reason so many little kids call them "Bonk Beds." If your older children have a bunk bed, put a gate up to block their bedroom on your co-op days. Smaller children can fall off the top or get caught between the guardrails.

Four Years

- *Scissors.* Of course, four-year-olds can use scissors under supervision. Even three-year-olds would do well to practice this fine motor skill. However, homemade haircuts are especially popular with this age group, so don't let the scissors out of your sight.
- *Staplers.* We know some kids this age who just love to make little books and staple the pages together. This is a great activity, but as with scissors, keep a close eye on the stapler. When it doesn't work like they want it to, they can get forceful with the obstinate device, which leads to injury, either to fingers or to the stapler.
- *Vitamins.* Iron pills are the most common cause of poisoning death in children under six. Some kids love vitamins especially the chewable ones taste like candy. So make sure all vitamins, child and adult versions, are out of sight and reach.

Safety Rules

At the start of a day when there are new children in your home, it's a good idea to set forth the rules so everyone knows what's expected of them. You won't want to overwhelm them with a huge list of rules they won't remember, but there will probably be a few rules that are musts at your house.

Every house has different safety issues, so think carefully about what potential hazards the kids might encounter. If you have pets, you'll need to tell the children whether or not they can touch the animals, where the animals are allowed to go, and how the pets should be treated. For example, specifically tell newcomers, "Don't touch Rover's tail."

But generally, tell the children to put things away when they're done with them, not to leave items on the stairs where others could trip on them, not to open cupboards or closets without permission, and to always wash their hands before they eat.

First Aid

Even when you are vigilant, accidents sometimes happen. Be sure to have your Contact List handy while you're watching the co-op kids. Should you not be able to reach a parent, handle the problem yourself, trusting your best judgment.

This section describes some of the most common injuries and sicknesses young children encounter. In a crisis, you'll find yourself much calmer if you have adequate first aid supplies on hand and know how to use them. It's a good idea to check your first aid kit every six months and restock items as needed.

In an emergency, follow these four steps:

1. **Assess the Situation.** Keep calm and try to figure out what happened, who is injured, and if there is any more danger you need to deal with.
2. **Think of Safety.** Don't put yourself at risk. As the caretaker, you need to be safe and able to take care of the children. Remove any source of danger and don't move the injured child.

3. **Treat Serious Conditions First.** Serious conditions include unconsciousness and severe bleeding. These can be life threatening. If more than one child is injured, go to the quiet one first. He may be unconscious.
4. **Get help.** Dial 911 and give them the following information:
    - Your telephone number
    - Your address and directions to your home
    - The name of the injured child and a summary of what happened

Bee Stings
1. If still lodged, scrape the stinger and poison sac with the thin edge of a credit card. Don't squeeze the stinger or sac.
2. Cool the area with ice or a cool, wet cloth.
3. Mix baking soda with water to make a thick paste. Apply the paste to the sting. When the paste has dried and the pain is relieved, just rinse the paste off with clear water.

Warning: If the child is allergic to bee stings, or if he has trouble breathing, call 911.

Nosebleeds
1. Have the child sit down with his head bent forward. Tell him to breathe through his mouth while you pinch the fleshy part of his nose.
2. Hold his nostrils together for about 10 minutes, with the child spitting out any blood that collects in his mouth.
3. After ten minutes, let go of his nose to see if it has stopped bleeding. If it hasn't, repeat step two for another ten minutes.
4. Once the bleeding has stopped, gently wash the area around his nose with a clean cloth and warm water. Dry the area, and then have the child sit quietly for about half an hour. Reading stories would be a good thing to do. Don't let him blow his nose.

Cuts & Abrasions
1. Use gauze pads or a warm wet washcloth to wash the abrasion. Remove any loose particles or dirt or gravel. Always wipe away from the wound so as not to introduce any dirt or bacteria to it.
2. Pat the wound dry with gauze and apply pressure until the bleeding stops.

3. Cover the abrasion with an adhesive bandage with a pad large enough to completely cover the abrasion.

Poisoning
Poisons include household chemicals, such as bleach, or by drinking alcohol or medicine, or eating pills or poisonous berries.
1. Calmly try to find out what the child has ingested, when she took it, and how much. Don't try to make her vomit.
2. Call the Poison Control Center at once (1-800-222-1222 in the United States). Follow their instructions.

Splinters
1. Clean the area around the splinter with soap and warm water. Pass the tweezers through a flame to sterilize them, and don't wipe off the soot.
2. Holding the tweezers as closely to the skin as possible, pull the splinter out.
3. Squeeze the wound to make it bleed. This expunges any tiny objects still lodged inside.
4. Cover the wound with an adhesive bandage.

Foreign Objects
1. In the ear: Don't try to remove it. Call the child's doctor for instructions.
2. In the eye: Encourage the child to blink. If the foreign object doesn't dislodge itself, call the doctor.
3. In the nose: If the child puts something in his nose, tell him to breathe through his mouth and call the doctor.

Burns
1. Immediately cool the burn with cool water for at least ten minutes.
2. Remove the child's clothing once the burn has cooled. If any material is stuck to the skin, cut around it with a pair of scissors. Cool the burn again. Don't apply any creams or ointments to the burn.
3. Cover the burn loosely with gauze or a clean cloth.
4. If the burn is severe, call 911.

Choking
First of all, you need to be able to recognize the signs of choking, which include clutching at the throat, turning blue in the face, and the

inability to speak or breath.

1. Tell the child to cough. If the blockage doesn't clear, move on to Step 2.
2. Stand or kneel behind the child. Wrap your arms around his abdomen just above the line of the hips. Make a fist with one hand and place the thumb side of your fist against the middle of his abdomen, just above his navel.
3. Grasping your fist with your other hand, press into his abdomen with a quick, upward motion.
4. If you can't clear the blockage in this manner, call 911. Repeat steps 2 and 3 until help arrives.

Head Injuries

Toddlers are especially notorious for hurting their heads. Most of their head bonks and bangs can be remedied with a kiss and some sympathy. We've found that it's wise to keep an ice pack on hand for such moments. Even if it doesn't bruise, an ice pack can show the child that you truly care. One wise mother of six told us that she keeps a zippered plastic bag of unpopped popcorn in the freezer for just such moments. Of course, you wouldn't want to hand the bag to a small child who would try to eat the popcorn, but for a four-year-old it would be just right.

When a child complains that he's hurt his head, ask him what happened and observe him

---

First Aid Kit Contents

- Adhesive bandages
- Gauze pads
- Eye pad with bandage
- Sterile non-adhesive pad
- Sterile dressing with bandage
- Small conforming (Ace) bandage
- Crepe roller bandage with securing clip
- Folded triangular bandage
- Hypoallergenic tape
- Safety pins
- Tweezers
- Scissors

closely for a while. If he fell from his own height or higher, chances are greater that he could have a concussion.

If you notice any of the following symptoms, call the doctor or 911:

- Loss of consciousness
- A headache that lasts more than an hour (a young child may cry and hold his head)
- Difficulty rousing from sleep
- Vomiting
- Oozing of blood or water from ears or nose
- Bruising around the eyes or behind the ears
- Depression or indentation in the skull
- Strange speech or behavior
- Persistent dizziness
- Seizures
- Unequal pupil size
- Unusual paleness

When Illness Strikes

If a mother knows her child is ill, she shouldn't bring the child to your house. Nonetheless, sometimes the child won't show any symptoms until two or three hours into a co-op session. The following tips should help you get through a morning or afternoon with a sick child who is not your own.

Once you realize that one of the children in your care is not feeling well, do your best to keep him from coughing on other children. Perhaps you could create a little bed with a blanket and pillow on the sofa, and settle the ill child there with some books or quiet toys.

When a child feels warm to the touch, take his temperature. Most doctors don't recommend administering acetaminophen (Tylenol) unless the temperature has reached 103 degrees. For a low-grade fever, just help the child get comfortable and offer him water so he doesn't get dehydrated.

If a child vomits, try to settle him down and help him feel safe. Vomiting can be a scary experience to young children. Help him wash out his mouth and get him comfortable with a bowl to cradle in his arms. He can use the bowl to vomit into next time, so he doesn't feel that he has to run to the bathroom. If the child has diarrhea and has a hard time making it to the bathroom, let him wear a pull-up or diaper so he won't worry so much.

For coughing, hand the child a tissue and show him how to cough into it. Sometimes the hum of a humidifier can soothe a troubled child who is missing his mother. It wouldn't hurt to set it up next to the sofa.

Do your best to stay cheerful. Reading stories or singing happy songs may ease the child's mind. It's not fun to be sick when your mother is away.

CHAPTER 18
IDEAS FOR EVENING ACTIVITIES, DINNERS & MOVIES

So it's your night to host the weekend co-op while all the other co-op couples enjoy a night on the town. Your children have high hopes for the evening. They've been waiting weeks for their turn to have all their friends over, and you don't want to disappoint.

The good news is that the kids are going to have a great time no matter what. They're happy just to have their friends nearby. But you can make it extra special and easy on everyone if you have a plan for the evening. It doesn't need to be elaborate to be fun. In fact, we've found that simple is always better because you'll be less stressed and more likely to enjoy yourself. Remember, your attitude is contagious and always rubs off on those within your home.

For a successful evening, you usually need three components: dinner, an activity, and a movie. This chapter is a resource for you in coming up with your plan for pleasing everyone involved.

Dinner Recipes

Warning: Dinner for a big group of children can get crazy. But if you treat this dinner differently than you treat everyday dinners, you'll find that you can cut down on messes, complaints, and general trauma.

First of all, consider the seating. Your table may be too small to accommodate all the children, so you'll have to get creative. You could have the children eat in shifts. If the weather is nice, you could spread an old quilt out on the patio or in the grass and let them have a picnic. Or if you have a child-sized table you could pull it into the kitchen for additional seating.

We've found that it's best for the adults to not eat at the same time as the children so that all adult hands are available to help. Besides, you'd probably be about three bites into your meal when the first preschooler announces that he's done.

The second consideration is the menu. We always try to serve very kid-friendly meals when it's our weekend shift because children have such varied tastes. Of course, the following menus and recipes are not fool proof; we're sure you'll run into a child here and there who is just downright picky. But these dinners are sure to please most of your crowd.

Whether or not to serve dessert should be something your co-op discusses when you come up with your rules. We usually skip the sweets but serve popcorn later on in the evening when we watch the movie.

The following eight menus should give you some ideas. These are menus we've successfully used with groups of children. At your initial planning meeting, remember to find out if any of the children have food allergies, and mothers of allergic children should be proactive in providing food ideas and recipes to the other members of the co-op. Recipes for italicized items are included later in this chapter. Bon Appétit!

Menu #1
Texas Beef Skillet (page 144)
Apple Slices
Corn (not on the cob)

Menu #2
Sloppy Joes (page 144)
Vegetables with Dip
Oven-Baked Fries (page 145)

Menu #3
Creamy Chicken and Rice (pages 144-145)
Green Beans
Rolls

Menu #4
Hot Dogs
Edamame*
Oven-Baked Fries (page 145)
Edamame is soybeans in the pod. You can find them in the frozen foods section of the grocery store. Most kids love these little beans. You can find them in the pods or already shelled. If you have a choice, buy the ones in the pods because kids inexplicably enjoy prying the pods open with their little fingers.

Menu #5
Taco Stacks (page 145)
Sliced Fruit

Menu #6
Pancakes (page 146)
Sausage or Bacon
Peaches or Pears

Menu #7
Mini Pizzas (page 145)
Breadsticks or Rolls
Veggies and Dip

Menu #8
Alphabet Soup (page 146)
Grilled Cheese Sandwiches

Texas Beef Skillet

1 lb. ground beef
¾ c. chopped onion
1 (16 oz.) can diced tomatoes
1 (15 oz.) can red kidney beans
½ cup white rice
½ cup water
3 Tbs. chopped green pepper
1 ½ tsp. chili powder
1 tsp. garlic salt
¾ shredded cheddar or American cheese
Tortilla or corn chips

In skillet, cook ground beef and onion until meat is browned and onion is tender. Drain off fat. Stir in undrained tomatoes, undrained beans, rice, water, green pepper, chili powder, and garlic salt. Bring to boiling; reduce heat. Cover and simmer for 20 minutes, stirring occasionally. Top meat mixture with shredded cheese. Cover and heat about 3 minutes, or until cheese melts. Serve over chips. Makes 6 generous adult-size servings.

Sloppy Joes

1 lb. ground beef
1 small onion

Brown above ingredients, drain fat, and add the following:

1 ½ tsp. dry mustard
1 can chicken gumbo soup
½ tsp Worcestershire sauce
¾ cup catsup

Simmer above ½ hour and serve in hamburger buns.

Or

Buy one of those packets of Sloppy Joe seasoning and follow the directions.

Creamy Chicken and Rice

1 ½ cups sour cream
2 cans cream of chicken soup

2 ½ cups cooked shredded chicken
2 cups cooked rice
2 cups crushed Ritz crackers
1 stick margarine, melted

In a bowl, combine sour cream and soup. Stir in chicken and cooked rice. Pour into a greased 13x9 pan. Combine the crumbs and butter; sprinkle over top. Bake, uncovered, at 350 degrees for 25-30 minutes.

Mini Pizzas
Mini bagels or English muffins
Can of pizza sauce
Mozzarella cheese
Pizza toppings

Spread a spoonful or two of pizza sauce on each bagel. Sprinkle cheese and toppings on top and bake in a 350-degree oven until cheese is melted and bubbly.

Note: Kids love to design and make their own pizzas.

Oven-Baked Fries
3 large potatoes
1-3 Tbs. olive oil or vegetable oil
salt and pepper, to taste

Preheat oven to 400 degrees. Scrub potatoes and cut into French fry-sized pieces. Put them in a bowl and toss them with oil so that each piece is coated. Spread them on greased cookie sheets, one layer thick, and sprinkle them with salt and pepper. Bake about 35-40 minutes.

Taco Stacks
1 lb. ground beef
1 packet taco seasoning
Shredded lettuce
Shredded cheddar cheese
Chopped tomatoes
Sour cream
Guacamole
Salsa
Tortilla Chips

Prepare the ground beef with the taco seasoning packet, according to the directions. Put all the other ingredients in separate bowls on the table and allow the children to make their stacks, starting with tortilla chips on the bottom.

Pancakes
2 cups whole wheat flour
2 Tbs. sugar
4 tsp. baking powder
½ tsp. salt
2 eggs, beaten
2 cups milk
¼ cup cooking oil

In a mixing bowl, combine the dry ingredients. In another bowl, mix the wet ingredients. Add wet mixture to dry mixture all at once and stir until blended but still lumpy. Pour about ¼ cup of batter onto a hot, lightly greased skillet for standard pancakes and about 1 Tbs. batter for dollar-sized pancakes. Makes 18-20 standard pancakes or about 70 dollar-sized.

Alphabet Soup
4 chicken breasts
3-4 cups chopped carrots
3-4 cups cubed potatoes
2 celery sticks, chopped fine
1 large onion, chopped fine
1 large pot of water
7 bouillon cubes
Alphabet pasta

Add bouillon cubes and chicken to water. Boil chicken until done, then remove chicken to cool and shred. Add vegetables to pot and boil until tender. Put chicken back in and add alphabet pasta. Cook until done. Add salt and pepper to taste. Makes a huge batch.

Activities

Now that dinner is over, it's time to have some fun before winding down for the movie. We've found that activities requiring energy are important at this stage of the game so everyone will be tired for the next stage.

Unless you have a well-contained back yard, it's risky to take a big group of kids outside in the evening because they can escape so quickly, so we've come up with some good indoor activities for you.

Dancing. This is Rachel and Ben's all-time favorite evening activity. The kids dance themselves ragged, it's good for their confidence, and it puts everyone in a good mood. All you need is an open space, some music, and a flashlight for the requisite spotlight. At the beginning, let everyone dance together. Don't forget to change the style of the music frequently. When they start to get tired, turn off the lights and get out the flashlight. Let them take turns dancing for each other and shining the spotlight on "The Star."

Sardines. This game is the opposite of Hide-and-Seek. At the beginning, only one person hides. Then everyone else goes to find him. When they find him, instead of shouting, they quietly hide with him. The last person to find the group, by then all squished together like sardines, is the first person to hide next time. Very young children will find this scary, especially if you play in the dark, so pair them up with older children.

Charades. Split the group into two teams and have one adult sit with each group. The adults whisper words or phrases to the children as they take turns acting for their own teams. Try to think of ideas that will really get them moving like pretending to be a horse or marching in a parade.

Party Games. Your evening will really feel like a party if you use traditional birthday party games for your activity. Musical Chairs, Pin the Tail, and Duck Duck Goose are fun and can be managed in a single room with lots of kids.

Sing Along. Singing can make for a great activity, especially if the songs have actions to them. Think of camp songs you learned as a child and teach them to the group. Bring out the old guitar if you're feeling up to it. Nursery songs and songs they've learned at church are fun, too. After you sing a few, usually one of the kids will volunteer to teach one she learned at preschool that week.

Relays. If you're in desperate need of getting some energy burned out of the kids, try this trick. "Spencer, run upstairs and touch the doorknob to the bathroom, then run downstairs and touch the purple chair in the living room, then come back and slap my hand." It's amazing how long this will keep them going, and all you have to do is sit there and come up with the course. You can send two at a time or have some of them monitor to make sure they touch all the right objects.

Making Statues. Pair the children off. One child is the sculptor and one is the clay. The clay sits in a lump on the floor and must hold each pose the sculptor puts him in. If the sculptor raises the other child's hand up, the hand must remain up. After the statues are complete, they shake themselves off and switch jobs.

Mime Talent Show. Again, the flashlight would be a good idea. Each child is assigned a talent for the show: magic tricks, singing, dancing, juggling, acrobatics, etc. Then they perform their talent with no props and no sounds, sort of like a mime. The other children have to guess what the talent is. They might want to try this several times until they get to perform all the different talents.

Movie Time

Now that they're fed and worn out, it's time to pull out the blankets and pillows and get comfortable. Chances are good they'll fall asleep in front of a great kid flick. If you were planning on serving popcorn, this is the time.

There are many great movies for kids out there, but some are not so great. While many movies are made by reputable children's film companies, they can cross the line. We've weeded out questionable movies and have included a list of tried-and-true, wholesome family movies.

Here's a list of some of the greats. Don't skip the oldies just because your kids have only seen the bright and ultra-stimulating new Disney movies. A five-year-old friend of ours, Tyler, adores *Bedknobs and*

Broomsticks, and one group of neighborhood co-op children we know just loves *The Sound of Music.* Introduce the kids in your co-op group to some of your old favorites.

The Absent-Minded Professor, 1961
The Adventures of Milo and Otis, 1989
An American Tail, 1986
Anne of Green Gables, 1985
The Aristocats, 1970
Babe, 1995
Bambi, 1942
Beauty and the Beast, 1991
Bedknobs and Broomsticks, 1971
The Borrowers, 1973
A Christmas Carol, 1984
Cinderella, 1950
Despicable Me, 2010
Escape to Witch Mountain, 1975
Finding Nemo, 2003
Freaky Friday, 1976
The Great Mouse Detective, 1986
Heidi, 1965
How the Grinch Stole Christmas, 1965
The Incredible Journey, 1963
The Incredibles, 2004
It's the Great Pumpkin, Charlie Brown, 1966
Lady and the Tramp, 1955
The Land Before Time, 1988
The Lion King, 1994
The Lion, the Witch, and the Wardrobe, 1979
The Little Mermaid, 1989
A Little Princess, 1995
The Lorax, 2012
The Many Adventures of Winnie the Pooh, 1977
Mary Poppins, 1964
Monsters, Inc., 2001
The Muppet Movie, 1979
The Muppets Take Manhattan, 1984
Nim's Island, 2008
Old Yeller, 1957
One Hundred and One Dalmatians, 1961
Over the Hedge, 2006

The Parent Trap, 1961
Pete's Dragon, 1977
Peter and the Wolf, 1946
Peter Pan, 1960
Pinocchio, 1940
Princess and the Frog, 2009
The Red Balloon, 1956
Sleeping Beauty, 1959
Snow White and the Seven Dwarfs, 1937
Song of the South, 1946
The Sound of Music, 1965
Stuart Little, 1999
Tangled, 2010
Tin Toy, 1988
Toy Story, 1995
Toy Story 2, 1999
The Velveteen Rabbit, 1984
Willy Wonka and the Chocolate Factory, 1971
The Wind in the Willows, 1983
Winnie the Pooh and the Honey Tree, 1965
Winnie the Pooh and Tigger Too!, 1974
The Wizard of Oz, 1939
The Yearling, 1946
You're in Love, Charlie Brown, 1967

The End of the Evening

The movie ends to the sounds of heavy breathing. About half of them are asleep, but the parents haven't begun to arrive. This is the time to pull out a stack of picture books and read in that voice you use when you try to induce sleep.

Soon the happy parents arrive and you help carry the sleeping ones out to the car. Everyone is happy. Those parents will go home to their clean homes and tuck their children into bed.

You tuck your own sleepy, satisfied children into bed, and while you vacuum the popcorn from the carpet you smile because the upcoming weekends will soon be yours to enjoy.

CONCLUSION

What is babysitting co-op really all about? It's about enhancing family relationships. The information and tools provided within this book all serve the same purpose, which is to help you find time to rejuvenate, gain perspective, and rediscover the joys of parenting. Regardless of our family backgrounds, financial status or size and shape, we all share the same dreams and desires. We all long to make our homes and families the best they can be. We hope that babysitting co-op can assist you in creating those positive changes for your family and yourself.

Along the way, we hope that you also enjoy the benefits of developing an extraordinary network of friends and circle of playmates for your children. Many of the adults that you interact with during these years will turn out to be lifelong friends. They'll be people who've possibly lent you a shoulder to cry on, have shared in your victories of potty training or realized that it's time for some overdue adult time and taken you to your favorite restaurant. Your children's friendships won't end once they rotate out of babysitting co-op either. Rather, they'll see each other in the halls at school and laugh about the times they spent playing tag in the yard or dressing-up in ball gowns while living the life of a royal princess.

True joy does not come from the things that we give our children, but rather from the time that we spend with them. And, while we may only hold the hands of our children for a few short years, it is our influence that will be felt for a lifetime. Now that you have a program in place that enables you to renew your energy stores and your spirit, you'll have more to give and the giving will be even sweeter.

Think of the priceless experience one girl recalls when her mother was able to give her some of the very best she had to offer while confidently knowing her other children were being watched by trusted co-op friends:

"When I was a young girl, I recall seeing my mother standing on the blacktop of my elementary school. I did not realize initially why she was there, nor do I remember what she told my teacher. What I did quickly discover was that my mom was taking me out of school early that day for no particular reason at all. Shortly after we left the school, mom pulled out a bag and told me that we were going to go swimming together at her health club. Just the two of us! This meant the world to me because I was the fourth child in a line of six. Spending one-on-one time with my mother was a rare experience. We spent that entire afternoon playing in the pool and strengthening the bonds of friendship and love. That afternoon was a magical one and one that I will always treasure."

INDEX

ABOUT THE AUTHORS

Samantha Fogg Nielsen graduated from George Mason University with a B.A. in Interpersonal Communications, and embraces the belief that building and maintaining exceptional relationships is essential to personal happiness. Samantha is a stay-at-home mom who owns and manages a successful retail business part-time and volunteers extensively within the local schools, her church organization, and community. As a public speaker, Samantha has addressed various parenting organizations about babysitting co-ops as well as conducted interviews with local news affiliates and newspapers. Samantha lives in Phoenix, Arizona, with her husband, Jeff, and their three children. You can reach Samantha at Samanthanielsen@yahoo.com.

Rachel Tolman Terry is the author of *Sister WhoDat, NY Agent* and *Tolman Hall* homeschool guides as well as numerous magazine articles. She lives in Lincoln, Nebraska, and enjoys traveling with her husband and three children. Rachel holds a B.A. in English from Brigham Young University and has been freelance writing during her kids' naps and activities since before they could crawl. You can find her online at www. racheltolmanterry.com or follow her on Twitter @_rachelterry_.

Made in the USA
Coppell, TX
20 January 2022

71994960R00096